W9-BKX-865

SUMMER SLOW COOKER

TASTE OF HOME BOOKS • RDA ENTHUSIAST BRANDS, LLC • MILWAUKEE, WI

Taste of Home

1610 N. 2nd St., Suite 102, Milwaukee WI 53212-3906

International Standard Book Number:
978-1-61765-774-0

Library of Congress Control Number:
2017963401

Component Number:
116000238H

Cover Photographer: Dan Roberts
Set Stylist: Dee Dee Jacq
Food Stylist: Shanon Roum

Pictured on front cover:
Brisket Sliders with Caramelized Onions, page 49

Pictured on title page:
Secret's in the Sauce BBQ Ribs, page 72

Pictured on back cover (from top):
Cranberry Hot Wings, page 21
Busy-Day Chicken Fajitas, page 60
Slow Cooker Berry Cobbler, page 99
Denver Omelet Frittata, page 31

Printed in U.S.A.
1 3 5 7 9 10 8 6 4 2

LIME CHICKEN TACOS, PAGE 65

TABLE OF CONTENTS

GET SOCIAL WITH US!

Like Us
facebook.com/tasteofhome

Follow Us
@tasteofhome

Pin Us
pinterest.com/taste_of_home

Tweet Us
twitter.com/tasteofhome

To find a recipe
tasteofhome.com

To submit a recipe
tasteofhome.com/submit

To find out about other *Taste of Home* products
shoptasteofhome.com

KEEP YOUR COOL THIS SUMMER

Dig in! Summer's here and that means it's time to enjoy barbecued classics, berry delights and fresh produce from the farmer's market. And if you're anything like millions of other family cooks, the last thing you want to do on a sweltering day is turn on the oven and heat up the kitchen for dinner. With **Taste of Home Summer Slow Cooker,** you don't have to. It's time to kick back, relax and let your slow cooker do the work!

Today's cooks are savvy about grabbing their slow cookers in the warm-weather months to free up time, keep the house cool, and dish up all those can't-do-withouts—and they're sharing their favorite summertime dishes here.

When the mercury rises, turn to entrees such as Slow Cooker Tropical Pork Chops (page 63), Lime Chicken Tacos (page 65) and Farm-Style BBQ Ribs (page 69). These summer specialties simmer on their own so you can head out for fun in the sun without worrying about dinner.

Going to a backyard barbecue, family picnic or block party? Your slow cooker is the perfect travel partner. Wow the crowd with Slow Cooker BBQ Baked Beans (page 85), Potluck Macaroni & Cheese (page 87) or Parsley Smashed Potatoes (page 90). Poolside nibbles are a snap, too, with appetizers and bites like refreshing Asian Wraps (page 11), Healthy Greek Bean Dip (page 13) and Slow-Cooked Peach Salsa (page 17).

What would summer be without fresh fruit ? Indulge your sweet tooth with Slow Cooker Key Lime Fondue (page 104), Blueberry Cobbler (page 106) and Strawberry-Banana Pudding Cake (page 108). You'll find these treats and 23 others in the chapter "Desserts & Snacks."

So hit the beach, take a stroll, go for a swim and simply enjoy everything this fantastic season has to offer. With your copy of **Summer Slow Cooker,** it's never been easier or more delicious!

AT-A-GLANCE EASE

(5)INGREDIENTS Look for this icon alongside recipes that call for only 5 or fewer ingredients, not including water, salt, pepper, oils or optional ingredients.

SLOW COOKER 101: COOKING WITH CONFIDENCE

Follow these tips for slow-cooking success every time.

PLAN AHEAD TO PREP AND GO. In most cases, you can prepare and load ingredients into the slow cooker insert beforehand and store it in the refrigerator overnight. But an insert can crack if exposed to rapid temperature changes. If your insert is cold, take it out of the refrigerator and let it sit just long enough to reach room temperature before placing it in the slow cooker.

USE THAWED INGREDIENTS. Although throwing frozen chicken breasts into the slow cooker may seem easy, it's not a smart shortcut. Foods thawing inside the slow cooker can create the ideal environment for bacteria to grow, so thaw frozen meat and veggies ahead of time. The exception is when you're using a prepackaged slow cooker meal kit with written instructions to follow.

GET HELP FROM FOIL. Some recipes in this book call for a coil or sling of aluminum foil. Here's why:

► A coil acts as a rack to aid in cooking and prevent scorching of dishes such as Denver Omelet Frittata (page 31). To make a coil, layer two 24-in.-long pieces of heavy-duty foil. Starting with the long side, fold foil to create a 1-in.-wide strip. Shape strip into a coil. Set coil on bottom of slow cooker.

► A sling helps you lift heavy foods, such as Cheesy Turkey Meat Loaf (page 67), out of the crock with ease. To make a sling, fold one or more pieces of heavy-duty foil into strips. Place on bottom and up sides of the slow cooker; coat with cooking spray or use as directed.

TAKE TIME TO BROWN. Give yourself a few extra minutes to brown your meat in a skillet before placing in the slow cooker. Doing this will add rich color and more flavor to the finished dish.

KEEP THE LID CLOSED. It's tempting to lift the lid and check on your meal's progress, but resist the urge. For every time you open the lid, you'll have to add as much as 30 minutes to the total cooking time.

ADJUST COOK TIME AS NEEDED. Live at a high altitude? Slow cooking will take longer. Add about 30 minutes for each hour of cooking the recipe calls for. And legumes will take roughly twice as long.

Want your food done sooner? Cooking 1 hour on high is roughly equal to 2 hours on low, so adjust the temperature to suit your schedule.

BUYING & MAINTAINING YOUR SLOW COOKER

If you're in the market for a slow cooker, there are a lot to choose from, ranging from about $20 to over $200. You may eventually own slow cookers in different sizes, but to start, think about what you'll be using the cooker for to decide which one is best for you. To learn more about specific models, check out product reviews online or in reputable consumer magazines. Consider:

SIZE: Slow cookers are available in sizes from 1½ to 7 quarts. Choose the size that's appropriate for your family.

SLOW COOKER SIZE

HOUSEHOLD SIZE	SLOW COOKER CAPACITY
1 person	1½ quarts
2 people	2 to 3½ quarts
3 or 4 people	3½ to 4½ quarts
4 or 5 people	4½ to 5 quarts
6 or more people	5 to 7 quarts

SHAPE: If you're going to be using your cooker to make roasts, an oval cooker is probably best. Round cookers are great for soups and stews.

SETTINGS: Most slow cookers have at least two settings: low (about 180°) and high (about 280°). Some models also have a keep-warm setting, which is useful if you plan to use yours for serving at buffets or potlucks. You might want a slow cooker that automatically switches to the keep-warm setting after the cooking time has elapsed; this provides added convenience and helps you avoid overcooking the food while you're away from home.

Note that most recipes provide a range of cooking times to account for variables such as the thickness of a cut of meat, the fullness of the slow cooker, and the desired finished temperature of the food. As you grow familiar with your new slow cooker, you'll be able to judge which end of the time range to use.

INSERT: Most slow cooker inserts are ceramic, but some pricier models have aluminum inserts that let you brown meats without dirtying an extra pan. For convenience, look for inserts that are dishwasher-safe.

SLOW COOKER BEEF TOSTADAS, PAGE 57

CLEANING A SLOW COOKER

- Removable stoneware inserts make cleanup a breeze. Be sure to cool the insert before rinsing or cleaning with water to avoid cracking. Don't immerse the metal base unit in water. Clean it with a damp sponge.
- Wash the insert in the dishwasher or in warm soapy water. Avoid using abrasive cleansers since they may scratch the stoneware or metal.
- To remove mineral stains on a ceramic insert, fill the cooker with hot water and 1 cup white vinegar; cover. Set the control to high and "cook" for 2 hours. Discard liquid, and when cool, wash with hot, sudsy water. Rinse well and dry.
- To remove water marks from a crockery insert, rub the surface with vegetable oil and allow to stand for 2 hours before washing with hot, sudsy water.

SLOW COOKER TEMPERATURE CHECK

New slow cookers heat up more quickly than older ones. If you have an older model and a recipe directs you to cook on low, try cooking on high for the first hour to ensure food safety. Older cookers may lose their efficiency, so it's a good idea to run regular checks to make sure they're reaching safe cooking temperatures.

To be considered safe, a slow cooker must be able to cook slow enough that it can be left unattended, yet fast enough to keep the food at a proper temperature. Here's how to check your slow cooker:

1. Fill the slow cooker ½ to ⅔ full with room-temperature water.
2. Cover; heat on low for 8 hours.
3. Use a thermometer to check the temperature of the water. (Work quickly—the temperature can drop once the lid is removed.)
4. The temperature should be at least 185°. If it's too hot, a meal cooked for 8 hours would likely be overdone. If the temperature is below 185°, the slow cooker will not cook food safely, and you should replace it.

PREPARING FOODS FOR THE SLOW COOKER

BEANS. Soak dried beans prior to cooking. Soak them overnight, or place them in a Dutch oven and add water to cover by 2 inches. Bring to a boil; boil for 2 minutes. Remove from heat, cover, and let stand for 1-4 hours. Drain and rinse beans, discarding the liquid. Lentils and split peas do not need soaking. Add any sugar, salt and acidic ingredients (such as vinegar) after the beans are fully cooked; they interfere with the beans' ability to cook.

DAIRY. Milk-based products tend to break down during slow cooking. Add items like milk, cream, sour cream or cream cheese during the last hour of cooking. Add cheese near the very end of the cooking time.

FISH & SEAFOOD. Fish and seafood can break down if cooked too long. Add them to the slow cooker toward the end of the cooking time.

MEAT. It's not necessary to brown meat before adding it to the slow cooker, but browning adds to the meat's flavor and appearance and allows you to drain off the fat. Cut roasts over 3 pounds in half to ensure even cooking. Trim excess fat from the outside of the meat. Fat retains heat, and large amounts of fat can raise the temperature of the cooking liquid, causing the meat to overcook.

OATS. Quick-cooking and old-fashioned oats are often interchangeable in recipes, but old-fashioned oats hold up better in the slow cooker.

PASTA. If added to a slow cooker when dry, pasta gets sticky. Instead, cook pasta according to package directions and stir into the slow cooker just before serving. Small pastas (such as orzo and ditalini) may be cooked in the slow cooker; to keep them from becoming mushy, add during the last hour or so of cooking.

RICE. Converted rice is ideal for all-day cooking. If using instant rice, add it during the last 30 minutes of cooking.

VEGETABLES. Firm vegetables, like potatoes and carrots, tend to cook more slowly than meat. Cut these into uniform pieces and place on the bottom and around the sides of the slow cooker. Place the meat over the vegetables. Tender vegetables, like peas and zucchini, should be added during the last 15-60 minutes of cooking.

SAUSAGE WITH JALAPENO POTATOES, PAGE 62

CONVERTING RECIPES FOR THE SLOW COOKER

Almost any recipe that bakes in the oven or simmers on the stovetop can be converted for the slow cooker. Here are some guidelines.

- Select recipes that simmer for at least 45 minutes. Good choices are soups, stews, pot roasts, chili and one-dish meals.
- Look for a slow cooker recipe that's similar to the one you want to convert. Note the quantity and size of the meat and vegetables, heat setting and cooking time.
- There's no evaporation from a slow cooker, so if a recipe calls for liquid, you'll need to use less. If a recipe calls for 6 to 8 cups of water, start with 5 cups. But if the recipe doesn't call for any liquid, add about ½ cup of water, broth or juice—all slow cooker recipes should include some liquid.

COOK TIMES

CONVENTIONAL OVEN	SLOW COOKER
15 to 30 minutes	Low: 4 to 6 hours High: 1½ to 2 hours
35 to 45 minutes	Low: 6 to 8 hours High: 3 to 4 hours
50 minutes or more	Low: 8 to 10 hours High: 4 to 6 hours

TOP 10 TIPS FOR SLOW COOKING

READ THE RECIPE FIRST. Not only will this ensure you have all the ingredients on hand, but reading the recipe allows you to consider and adjust time elements. If you live at a high altitude, for instance, you'll need to adjust the cooking time accordingly.

CHOOSE THE RIGHT CUT OF MEAT. Lower-cost cuts work better than higher-priced lean cuts. Trim excess fat from the outside, but look for good marbling on the inside. It will break down during cooking and make the meat tender.

MAKE SURE THE LID FITS. Be sure the lid is secure, not tilted or askew. Steam held in during cooking creates a seal.

GO EASY ON THE ALCOHOL. Alcohol won't evaporate from the slow cooker, so use sparingly. If you brown the meat, use wine to deglaze the pan, then pour the liquid into the slow cooker. This will burn off the alcohol but leave the flavor.

DON'T OVERFILL OR UNDERFILL. Fill the slow cooker between ½ and ⅔ full. Less than ½ full, the food may burn. More than ⅔ full, the food may not cook completely.

DON'T LET IT GET COLD. If you won't be home when the cooking time is up, be sure the cooker will switch itself to Warm. Temperatures between 40-140° allow bacteria to thrive.

HALVE THE TIME BY DOUBLING SETTING. On most models, Low is 170° and High is 280°. For many recipes, cranking up the heat will cut down the cook time.

DON'T PEEK! Remember that each time you lift the lid, you'll need to add 15-30 minutes of cooking time. Open only when instructed.

AVOID TEMPERATURE SHOCKS. If your cooker has a ceramic insert, put a dishtowel on a cold work surface before setting the hot insert down. Do not preheat your cooker. A cold insert should always be put into a cold base.

KEEP IT FRESH. Do not use your slow cooker to reheat food. Slow-cooked meals reheat well in the microwave, an oven or on the stovetop.

APPETIZERS & MORE

Sliders, wraps and nachos from a slow cooker? You've got it! Hosting summer get-togethers is a snap when these mouthwatering bites are at the ready.

ASIAN WRAPS

ASIAN WRAPS

Talk about an impressive appetizer! Here's a light and refreshing version of a restaurant favorite. Don't be intimidated by working with rice paper. It's actually very easy to use. Instead of ordering Chinese, you'll be making these yourself.

—Melissa Hansen Milwaukee, WI

Prep: 30 min. • **Cook:** 3½ hours
Makes: 1 dozen

- **2 pounds boneless skinless chicken breast halves**
- **¼ cup reduced-sodium soy sauce**
- **¼ cup ketchup**
- **¼ cup honey**
- **2 tablespoons minced fresh gingerroot**
- **2 tablespoons sesame oil**
- **1 small onion, finely chopped**
- **2 tablespoons cornstarch**
- **2 tablespoons water**
- **12 round rice papers (8 inches)**
- **3 cups broccoli coleslaw mix**
- **¾ cup crispy chow mein noodles**

1. Place chicken in a 3-qt. slow cooker. In a small bowl, whisk soy sauce, ketchup, honey, ginger and oil; stir in onion. Pour over chicken. Cook, covered, on low 3-4 hours or until chicken is tender. Remove the chicken; shred with two forks and refrigerate until assembly.
2. Meanwhile, in a small bowl, mix the cornstarch and water until smooth; gradually stir into honey mixture. Cook, covered, on high 20-30 minutes or until sauce is thickened. Toss chicken with ¾ cup sauce; reserve the remaining sauce for serving.
3. Fill a large shallow dish partway with water. Dip a rice paper wrapper into water just until pliable, about 45 seconds (do not soften completely); allow excess water to drip off.
4. Place wrapper on a flat surface. Layer ¼ cup coleslaw, ⅓ cup chicken mixture and 1 tablespoon noodles across bottom third of wrapper. Fold in both sides of wrapper; fold bottom over filling, then roll up tightly. Place on a serving plate, seam side down. Repeat with remaining ingredients. Serve with reserved sauce.

MINI TERIYAKI TURKEY SANDWICHES

Preparing this pulled turkey is a breeze using a slow cooker. We love the delicious teriyaki sauce. Serving these snack-size sandwiches on lightly-toasted sweet dinner rolls is perfection made easy.

—Amanda Hoop Seaman, OH

Prep: 20 min. • **Cook:** 5½ hours
Makes: 20 servings

- **2 boneless skinless turkey breast halves (2 pounds each)**
- **⅔ cup packed brown sugar**
- **⅔ cup reduced-sodium soy sauce**
- **¼ cup cider vinegar**
- **3 garlic cloves, minced**
- **1 tablespoon minced fresh gingerroot**
- **½ teaspoon pepper**
- **2 tablespoons cornstarch**
- **2 tablespoons cold water**
- **20 Hawaiian sweet rolls**
- **2 tablespoons butter, melted**

1. Place turkey breast in a 5- or 6-qt. slow cooker. In a small bowl, combine brown sugar, soy sauce, vinegar, garlic, ginger and pepper; pour over turkey. Cook, covered, on low 5-6 hours or until meat is tender.
2. Remove turkey from slow cooker. In a small bowl, mix cornstarch and cold water until smooth; gradually stir into cooking liquid. When cool enough to handle, shred meat with two forks and return meat to the slow cooker. Cook, covered, on high 30-35 minutes or until sauce is thickened.
3. Preheat oven to 325°. Split rolls and brush cut sides with butter; place on an ungreased baking sheet, cut side up. Bake 8-10 minutes or until toasted and golden brown. Spoon ⅓ cup turkey mixture on roll bottoms. Replace tops.

TEST KITCHEN TIP

This sandwich recipe also works great with boneless, skinless chicken breasts. To spice things up, add crushed red pepper flakes or a few slices of fresh jalapeno pepper.

SLOW COOKER SWEET & SOUR MEATBALLS

These saucy meatballs are just as good in summer as in winter. I often make them with ground turkey.

—**Rachelle Stratton** Rock Springs, WY

Prep: 30 min. • **Cook:** 3 hours
Makes: 3 dozen

- **2 large eggs, lightly beaten**
- **¼ cup panko (Japanese) bread crumbs**
- **2 garlic cloves, minced**
- **2 teaspoons salt-free garlic herb seasoning blend**
- **½ teaspoon salt**
- **¼ teaspoon pepper**
- **2 pounds ground beef**
- **1 can (15 ounces) tomato sauce**
- **1 cup chicken broth**
- **1 bottle (12 ounces) chili sauce**
- **½ cup packed brown sugar**
- **½ cup cider or white vinegar**
- **1 green onion, thinly sliced**

1. Preheat oven to 375°. In a large bowl, combine the first six ingredients. Add beef; mix lightly but thoroughly. Shape into 1½-in. balls. Place meatballs on a greased rack in a 15x10x1-in. baking pan. Bake 15-20 minutes or until meatballs are lightly browned.

2. In large bowl, combine tomato sauce, broth, chili sauce, brown sugar and vinegar. Transfer meatballs to a 5-qt. slow cooker. Pour sauce over top. Cook, covered, on low for 3-4 hours or until meatballs are cooked through. To serve, sprinkle with green onion.

TEST KITCHEN TIP

To make meatballs the same size, pat the meat mixture into a 1-inch-thick rectangle. Cut the rectangle into the same number of squares as meatballs in the recipe. Gently roll each square into a ball.

HEALTHY GREEK BEAN DIP

Served warm or cold, this crowd-pleasing dip is a perfect match for fresh veggies, crackers or pita chips. We like it as an alternative to hummus, and it's on the table at all our summer get-togethers.
—**Kelly Silvers** Edmond, OK

Prep: 15 min. • **Cook:** 2 hours
Makes: 3 cups

- **2 cans (15 ounces each) cannellini beans, rinsed and drained**
- **¼ cup water**
- **¼ cup finely chopped roasted sweet red peppers**
- **2 tablespoons finely chopped red onion**
- **2 tablespoons olive oil**
- **2 tablespoons lemon juice**
- **1 tablespoon snipped fresh dill**
- **2 garlic cloves, minced**
- **¼ teaspoon salt**
- **¼ teaspoon pepper**
- **1 small cucumber, peeled, seeded and finely chopped**
- **½ cup fat-free plain Greek yogurt**
- **Additional snipped fresh dill**
- **Baked pita chips or assorted fresh vegetables**

Process the beans and water in a food processor until smooth. Transfer to a greased 1½-qt. slow cooker. Add the next eight ingredients. Cook, covered, on low until heated through, 2-3 hours. Stir in the cucumber and yogurt; cool slightly. Sprinkle with additional dill. Serve warm or cold with baked pita chips or assorted fresh vegetables.

To freeze: Omitting cucumber, yogurt and additional dill, freeze cooled dip in freezer containers. To use, thaw in the refrigerator overnight. To serve dip warm, heat through in a saucepan, stirring occasionally. Or serve cold. Stir cucumber and yogurt into finished dip; sprinkle with additional dill. Serve with baked pita chips or vegetables.

HEALTHY GREEK BEAN DIP

SLOW COOKER MARINATED MUSHROOMS

Here's a terrific, healthy addition to any buffet spread. Mushrooms and pearl onions seasoned with herbs, balsamic and red wine are terrific on their own or as a side dish alongside a tenderloin roast.
—**Courtney Wilson** Fresno, CA

Prep: 15 min. • **Cook:** 6 hours
Makes: 20 servings

- **2 pounds medium fresh mushrooms**
- **1 package (14.4 ounces) frozen pearl onions, thawed**
- **4 garlic cloves, minced**
- **2 cups reduced-sodium beef broth**
- **½ cup dry red wine**
- **3 tablespoons balsamic vinegar**
- **3 tablespoons olive oil**
- **1 teaspoon salt**
- **1 teaspoon dried basil**
- **½ teaspoon dried thyme**
- **½ teaspoon pepper**
- **¼ teaspoon crushed red pepper flakes**

Place mushrooms, onions and garlic in a 5- or 6-qt. slow cooker. In a small bowl, whisk remaining ingredients; pour over mushrooms. Cook, covered, on low until mushrooms are tender, 6-8 hours.

To freeze: Freeze cooled mushrooms and juices in freezer containers. To use, partially thaw in refrigerator overnight. Microwave, covered, on high in a microwave-safe dish until heated through, stirring gently and adding a little broth or water if necessary.

CREAMY ARTICHOKE DIP

This comforting dip is a family favorite. My sister got the recipe from a friend and passed it along to me. It's loaded with four types of cheese, artichoke hearts and just the right amount of spice.
—**Mary Spencer** Greendale, WI

Prep: 20 min. • **Cook:** 1 hour
Makes: 5 cups

- **2 cans (14 ounces each) water-packed artichoke hearts, rinsed, drained and coarsely chopped**
- **2 cups shredded part-skim mozzarella cheese**
- **1 package (8 ounces) cream cheese, cubed**
- **1 cup shredded Parmesan cheese**
- **½ cup mayonnaise**
- **½ cup shredded Swiss cheese**
- **2 tablespoons lemon juice**
- **2 tablespoons plain yogurt**
- **1 tablespoon seasoned salt**
- **1 tablespoon chopped seeded jalapeno pepper**
- **1 teaspoon garlic powder**
- **Tortilla chips**

In a 3-qt. slow cooker, combine the first 11 ingredients. Cover and cook on low for 1 hour or until heated through. Serve with tortilla chips.

Note: Wear disposable gloves when cutting hot peppers; the oils can burn skin. Avoid touching your face.

SWEET & TANGY CHICKEN WINGS

Here's a festive recipe that's perfect for parties. Start the wings before you prepare for guests, and in a few hours you'll have wonderful appetizers!
—**Ida Tuey** South Lyon, MI

Prep: 20 min. • **Cook:** 3¼ hours
Makes: about 2½ dozen

- **3 pounds chicken wingettes (about 30)**
- **½ teaspoon salt, divided**
- **Dash pepper**
- **1½ cups ketchup**
- **¼ cup packed brown sugar**
- **¼ cup red wine vinegar**
- **2 tablespoons Worcestershire sauce**
- **1 tablespoon Dijon mustard**
- **1 teaspoon minced garlic**
- **1 teaspoon liquid smoke, optional**
- **Sesame seeds, optional**

1. Sprinkle chicken with a dash of salt and pepper. Broil 4-6 in. from the heat for 5-10 minutes on each side or until golden brown. Transfer wings to a greased 5-qt. slow cooker.
2. Combine the ketchup, brown sugar, vinegar, Worcestershire sauce, mustard, garlic, liquid smoke if desired and the remaining salt; pour over wings. Toss to coat.
3. Cover and cook on low for 3¼ to 3¾ hours or until chicken juices run clear. Sprinkle with sesame seeds if desired.

Freeze option: Freeze cooled fully-cooked wings in freezer containers. To use, partially thaw in refrigerator overnight. Reheat wings in a foil-lined 15x10x1-in. baking pan in a preheated 325° oven until heated through, covering if necessary to prevent browning. Serve wings as directed.

SWEET & TANGY CHICKEN WINGS

SOUTHWESTERN PULLED PORK CROSTINI

SOUTHWESTERN PULLED PORK CROSTINI

For a unique take on crostini, try my hearty appetizers. The bites are spicy, sweet and salty, and the layers of salsa and sauce make the recipe even more special.
—Randy Cartwright Linden, WI

Prep: 45 min. • **Cook:** 6 hours
Makes: 32 appetizers

- **1 boneless pork shoulder butt roast (about 2 pounds)**
- **½ cup lime juice**
- **2 envelopes mesquite marinade mix**
- **¼ cup sugar**
- **¼ cup olive oil**

SALSA

- **1 cup frozen corn, thawed**
- **1 cup canned black beans, rinsed and drained**
- **1 small tomato, finely chopped**
- **2 tablespoons finely chopped seeded jalapeno pepper**
- **2 tablespoons lime juice**
- **2 tablespoons olive oil**
- **1½ teaspoons ground cumin**
- **1 teaspoon chili powder**
- **½ teaspoon salt**
- **¼ teaspoon crushed red pepper flakes**

SAUCE

- **1 can (4 ounces) chopped green chilies**
- **⅓ cup apricot preserves**
- **⅛ teaspoon salt**

CROSTINI

- **32 slices French bread baguette (¼ inch thick)**
- **¼ cup olive oil**
- **⅔ cup crumbled queso fresco or feta cheese**
- **Lime wedges, optional**

1. Place roast in a 3-qt. slow cooker. In a small bowl, whisk lime juice, marinade mix, sugar and oil until blended; pour over roast. Cook, covered, on low 6-8 hours or until meat is tender.
2. For salsa, in a small bowl, combine corn, beans, tomato and jalapeno. Stir in lime juice, oil and seasonings. In a small saucepan, combine sauce ingredients; cook and stir over low heat until blended.
3. For crostini, preheat broiler. Brush bread slices on both sides with oil; place on ungreased baking sheets. Broil 3-4 in. from heat 1-2 minutes on each side or until golden brown.
4. Remove roast from slow cooker; cool slightly. Shred pork with two forks. To serve, layer toasts with salsa, pork and cheese. Top with sauce. If desired, serve with lime wedges.

HAWAIIAN KIELBASA

Savory sausage teams up with juicy pineapple for a winning combination you can prep in a flash. The barbecue-style sauce is a sweet way to bring the flavors all together.
—Louise Kline Fort Myers, FL

Prep: 15 min. • **Cook:** 3 hours
Makes: 12 servings

- **2 pounds smoked kielbasa or Polish sausage, cut into 1-inch pieces**
- **1 can (20 ounces) unsweetened pineapple chunks, undrained**
- **½ cup ketchup**
- **2 tablespoons brown sugar**
- **2 tablespoons yellow mustard**
- **1 tablespoon cider vinegar**
- **¾ cup lemon-lime soda**
- **2 tablespoons cornstarch**
- **2 tablespoons cold water**

1. Place sausage in a 3- or 4-qt. slow cooker. Drain pineapple, reserving ¾ cup juice; set pineapple aside. In a small bowl, whisk the ketchup, brown sugar, mustard and vinegar. Stir in soda and reserved pineapple juice. Pour over the sausage; stir to coat. Cover and cook on low for 2-3 hours or until heated through.
2. Stir in pineapple. In a small bowl, combine cornstarch and water until smooth. Stir into slow cooker. Cover and cook 30 minutes longer or until sauce is thickened. Serve with toothpicks.

DID YOU KNOW?

Cider vinegar, made from apples, has a faint fruity flavor and is used in recipes where a slightly milder vinegar flavor is preferred. If a recipe doesn't specify which type of vinegar to use, try using cider vinegar for a hint of flavor, white vinegar if you are looking for a little more sharpness.

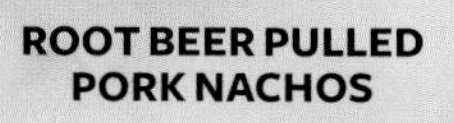

ROOT BEER PULLED PORK NACHOS

(5) INGREDIENTS

ROOT BEER PULLED PORK NACHOS

I count on my slow cooker to do the honors when I have a house full of summer guests. Teenagers especially love these full-flavored nachos, but no one guesses the secret ingredient is soda. Try cola, ginger ale or lemon-lime soda if you're not into root beer.

—**James Schend** Pleasant Prairie, WI

Prep: 20 min. • **Cook:** 8 hours
Makes: 12 servings

- **1 boneless pork shoulder butt roast (3 to 4 pounds)**
- **1 can (12 ounces) root beer**
- **12 cups tortilla chips**
- **2 cups shredded cheddar cheese**
- **2 medium tomatoes, chopped**
- **Pico de gallo, chopped green onions and sliced jalapeno peppers, optional**

1. In a 4- or 5-qt. slow cooker, combine pork roast and root beer. Cook, covered, on low until meat is tender, 8-9 hours.
2. Remove roast. When cool enough to handle, shred meat with two forks. Return to slow cooker; keep warm.
3. To serve, drain pork. Layer tortilla chips with pork, cheese, tomatoes and, if desired, optional toppings. Serve the nachos immediately.

TEST KITCHEN TIP

The cooked and cooled pork can be frozen in freezer containers for up to 4 months. Just be sure the cooking liquid covers the meat so it doesn't dry out. To use, partially thaw in the refrigerator overnight, then reheat in the microwave or on the stovetop. This recipe was tested with regular root beer, not diet or low-calorie.

SLOW-COOKED PEACH SALSA

SLOW-COOKED PEACH SALSA

Fresh peaches and tomatoes make my salsa a hands-down winner over store versions. As a treat, I give my co-workers several jars throughout the year.

—**Peggi Stahnke** Cleveland, OH

Prep: 20 min. • **Cook:** 3 hours + cooling
Makes: 11 cups

- **4 pounds tomatoes (about 12 medium), chopped**
- **1 medium onion, chopped**
- **4 jalapeno peppers, seeded and finely chopped**
- **½ to ⅔ cup packed brown sugar**
- **¼ cup minced fresh cilantro**
- **4 garlic cloves, minced**
- **1 teaspoon salt**
- **4 cups chopped peeled fresh peaches (about 4 medium), divided**
- **1 can (6 ounces) tomato paste**

1. In a 5-qt. slow cooker, combine the first seven ingredients; stir in 2 cups peaches. Cook, covered, on low 3-4 hours or until onion is tender.
2. Stir tomato paste and remaining peaches into slow cooker. Cool. Transfer to covered containers. (If freezing, use freezer-safe containers and fill to within ½ in. of tops.) Refrigerate up to 1 week or freeze up to 12 months. Thaw frozen salsa in refrigerator before serving.

Note: Wear disposable gloves when cutting hot peppers; the oils can burn skin. Avoid touching your face.

(5) INGREDIENTS

CRUNCHY CANDY CLUSTERS

Before I retired, I took these yummy peanut butter bites to work anytime there was a special occasion. They're so simple! I still make them for holidays because my family looks forward to the coated cereal and marshmallow clusters.

—Faye O'Bryan Owensboro, KY

Prep: 15 min. • **Cook:** 1 hour + standing
Makes: about 6½ dozen

- **2 pounds white candy coating, coarsely chopped**
- **1½ cups peanut butter**
- **½ teaspoon almond extract, optional**
- **4 cups Cap'n Crunch cereal**
- **4 cups crisp rice cereal**
- **4 cups miniature marshmallows**

1. Place candy coating in a 5-qt. slow cooker. Cover and cook on high for 1 hour. Add peanut butter. Stir in the extract if desired.
2. In a large bowl, combine the cereals and marshmallows. Add the peanut butter mixture and stir until the cereal mixture is well-coated. Drop by tablespoonfuls onto waxed paper. Let stand until set. Store the clusters at room temperature.

CORN CHIP CHILI CHEESE DIP

After trying to create a Mexican soup, I wound up with this outstanding dip. My husband and two young children love it, and so do guests at summer gatherings and fall football game days.

—Sandra Fick Lincoln, NE

Prep: 20 min. • **Cook:** 4½ hours
Makes: 8 cups

- **1 pound lean ground beef (90% lean)**
- **1 medium onion, chopped**
- **1 can (16 ounces) kidney beans, rinsed and drained**
- **1 can (15 ounces) black beans, rinsed and drained**
- **1 can (14½ ounces) diced tomatoes in sauce, undrained**
- **1 cup frozen corn, thawed**
- **¾ cup water**
- **1 can (2¼ ounces) sliced ripe olives, drained**
- **3 teaspoons chili powder**
- **½ teaspoon dried oregano**
- **½ teaspoon chipotle hot pepper sauce**
- **¼ teaspoon garlic powder**
- **¼ teaspoon ground cumin**
- **1 package (16 ounces) reduced-fat process cheese (Velveeta), cubed**
- **Corn chips or tortilla chips**

1. In a large skillet, cook beef and onion over medium heat 6-8 minutes or until beef is no longer pink and onion is tender, breaking up beef into crumbles; drain. Transfer to a 4-qt. slow cooker.
2. Stir in the beans, tomatoes, corn, water, olives, chili powder, oregano, pepper sauce, garlic powder and cumin. Cook, covered, on low 4-5 hours or until heated through.
3. Stir in cheese. Cook, covered, on low 30 minutes longer or until the cheese is melted. Serve with corn chips.

CORN CHIP CHILI CHEESE DIP

PULLED PORK DOUGHNUT HOLE SLIDERS

PULLED PORK DOUGHNUT HOLE SLIDERS

This slider recipe was created by accident when we had a surplus of root beer left over from a party. Now we can't have barbecue any other way!
—Eden Dranger Los Angeles, CA

Prep: 55 min. • **Cook:** 8 hours.
Makes: 5 dozen

- **1 bottle (2 liters) root beer**
- **1½ cups barbecue sauce**
- **1½ teaspoons salt**
- **1 teaspoon minced fresh gingerroot**
- **1 bone-in pork shoulder roast (about 3 pounds)**

SLAW

- **½ cup mayonnaise**
- **2 tablespoons white vinegar**
- **1 tablespoon maple syrup**
- **1 package (14 ounces) coleslaw mix**

ASSEMBLY

- **60 plain doughnut holes**
- **60 appetizer skewers**
- **Additional barbecue sauce, optional**

1. In a large saucepan, bring root beer to a boil. Reduce heat to medium-high; cook, uncovered, until liquid is reduced by half, 30-45 minutes. Transfer to a 5- or 6-qt. slow cooker. Stir in barbecue sauce, salt and ginger. Add the roast, turning to coat.
2. Cook, covered, on low until pork is tender, 8-10 hours. For slaw, in a large bowl, mix mayonnaise, vinegar and syrup. Stir in coleslaw mix. Refrigerate, covered, until flavors are blended, at least 1 hour.
3. Remove pork from slow cooker; skim fat from cooking juices. Remove meat from bones; shred with two forks. Return juices and pork to the slow cooker; heat mixture through.
4. To serve, cut doughnut holes in half; cut a thin slice off bottoms to level. Serve pork and slaw in doughnut holes; secure with skewers. If desired, serve sliders with additional barbecue sauce.

Freeze option: Freeze cooled pork mixture in freezer containers. To use, partially thaw in refrigerator overnight. Heat through in a covered saucepan, stirring gently.

BUFFALO WING DIP

If you like spice, you'll love this dip. It's super cheesy, full of rich flavor and really has that Buffalo wing taste!
***—Taste of Home* Test Kitchen**

Prep: 20 min. • **Cook:** 2 hours
Makes: 6 cups

- **2 packages (8 ounces each) cream cheese, softened**
- **½ cup ranch salad dressing**
- **½ cup sour cream**
- **5 tablespoons crumbled blue cheese**
- **2 cups shredded cooked chicken**
- **½ cup Buffalo wing sauce**
- **2 cups shredded cheddar cheese, divided**
- **1 green onion, sliced**
- **Tortilla chips**

1. In a small bowl, combine the cream cheese, dressing, sour cream and blue cheese. Transfer to a 3-qt. slow cooker. Layer with chicken, wing sauce and 1 cup cheese. Cover and cook on low for 2-3 hours or until heated through.
2. Sprinkle with remaining cheese and onion. Serve with tortilla chips.

PORK PICADILLO LETTUCE WRAPS

Warm pork and cool, crisp lettuce are a combination born in culinary heaven. My spin on a lettuce wrap is chock-full of scrumptious flavor and surprising spice.
—Janice Elder Charlotte, NC

Prep: 30 min. • **Cook:** 2½ hours.
Makes: 2 dozen

- **3 garlic cloves, minced**
- **1 tablespoon chili powder**
- **1 teaspoon salt**
- **½ teaspoon pumpkin pie spice**
- **½ teaspoon ground cumin**
- **½ teaspoon pepper**
- **2 pork tenderloins (1 pound each)**
- **1 large onion, chopped**
- **1 small Granny Smith apple, peeled and chopped**
- **1 small sweet red pepper, chopped**
- **1 can (10 ounces) diced tomatoes and green chilies, undrained**
- **½ cup golden raisins**
- **½ cup chopped pimiento-stuffed olives**
- **24 Bibb or Boston lettuce leaves**
- **¼ cup slivered almonds, toasted**

1. Mix garlic and seasonings; rub over pork. Transfer to a 5-qt. slow cooker. Add the onion, apple, sweet pepper and tomatoes. Cook, covered, on low for 2½ to 3 hours or until meat is tender.
2. Remove pork; cool slightly. Shred meat into bite-size pieces; return to slow cooker. Stir in raisins and olives; heat through. Serve in lettuce leaves; sprinkle with almonds.

HONEY & ALE PULLED CHICKEN SLIDERS

HONEY & ALE PULLED CHICKEN SLIDERS

Score big with your guests with a little bit of sweet heat! This recipe works well for a football party—the extra liquid in the slow cooker keeps it nice and juicy all day long.
—Julie Peterson Crofton, MD

Prep: 20 min. • **Cook:** 6 hours
Makes: 12 servings

- **¼ cup honey**
- **2 tablespoons cider vinegar**
- **2 tablespoons Sriracha Asian hot chili sauce**
- **1 tablespoon chili powder**
- **1 teaspoon smoked paprika**
- **1 teaspoon garlic powder**
- **1 teaspoon onion powder**
- **½ teaspoon salt**
- **2 pounds boneless skinless chicken thighs (about 8 thighs)**
- **¾ cup brown ale**
- **3 tablespoons cornstarch**
- **3 tablespoons water**
- **12 slider buns**
- **Sweet pickles and additional Sriracha sauce, optional**

1. In a 3- or 4-qt. slow cooker, combine the first eight ingredients. Add chicken and ale; toss to coat. Cook, covered, on low until chicken is tender, 6-8 hours. Remove the meat; when cool enough to handle, shred with two forks.
2. Strain cooking juices; skim the fat. Transfer juices to a small saucepan; bring to a boil. In a small bowl, mix cornstarch and water until smooth; stir into the saucepan. Return to a boil, stirring constantly; cook and stir until thickened, about 5 minutes. Add chicken to the sauce; toss to coat.
3. Serve on buns, with pickles and additional Sriracha sauce if desired.

TEST KITCHEN TIP

Look for a brown ale that packs a punch, and you'll have a fantastic crowd-pleasing meal that takes only about five minutes of active prep time before the chicken goes into the slow cooker. It's OK to be a little heavy-handed with the Sriracha if you love it spicy. And you can always squeeze on more after you assemble the sliders.

CRANBERRY HOT WINGS

Chicken wings get special treatment from cranberry sauce, a little citrus and a touch of hot sauce in this no-fuss recipe. The wings are a flavorful complement to all sorts of summer get-together dishes.
—**Robin Haas** Cranston, RI

Prep: 50 min. • **Cook:** 2 hours
Makes: about 2½ dozen

- 1 **can (14 ounces) jellied cranberry sauce, cubed**
- 2 **tablespoons ground mustard**
- 2 **tablespoons hot pepper sauce**
- 2 **tablespoons reduced-sodium soy sauce**
- 2 **tablespoons honey**
- 1 **tablespoon cider vinegar**
- 2 **teaspoons garlic powder**
- 1 **teaspoon grated orange peel**
- 3 **pounds chicken wings**
- **Blue cheese salad dressing and celery sticks**

1. In a 5-qt. slow cooker, combine the first eight ingredients. Cover and cook on low for 45 minutes or until cranberry sauce is melted.
2. Cut the wings into three sections; discard wing tip sections. Place wings on a greased broiler pan. Broil 4-6 in. from the heat for 15-20 minutes or until lightly browned, turning occasionally.
3. Transfer wings to slow cooker; toss to coat. Cover and cook on high for 2-3 hours or until tender. Serve with dressing and celery.

Note: Uncooked chicken wing sections (wingettes) may be substituted for whole chicken wings.

CRANBERRY HOT WINGS

ONE-BITE TAMALES

Clever little meatballs deliver the flavor and rich sauce of a traditional tamale in a bite-size portion. They're a delightfully different addition to any spread.
—**Dolores Jaycox** Gretna, LA

Prep: 40 min. • **Cook:** 3 hours 20 min.
Makes: about 5½ dozen

- 1¼ **cups cornmeal**
- ½ **cup all-purpose flour**
- 5¾ **cups V8 juice, divided**
- 4 **teaspoons chili powder, divided**
- 4 **teaspoons ground cumin, divided**
- 2 **teaspoons salt, divided**
- 1 **teaspoon garlic powder**
- ½ **to 1 teaspoon cayenne pepper**
- 1 **pound bulk spicy pork sausage**
- **Tortilla chip scoops**

1. Preheat oven to 350°. Mix cornmeal, flour, ¾ cup V8 juice, 2 teaspoons chili powder, 2 teaspoons cumin, 1 teaspoon salt, garlic powder and cayenne. Add the sausage; mix lightly but thoroughly. Shape into 1-in. balls.
2. Place meatballs on a greased rack in a 15x10-in. pan. Bake until cooked through, 20-25 minutes.
3. Meanwhile, in a 4-qt. slow cooker, mix remaining V8 juice, chili powder, cumin and salt. Gently stir in meatballs. Cook, covered, on low until heated through, 3-4 hours. Serve with tortilla chip scoops.

SLOW COOKER
SPINACH ARTICHOKE DIP

SPICY CHICKEN EGG ROLLS

One of my favorite slow cooker recipes is this impressive appetizer. It seems difficult, but the egg rolls come together quickly and easily. We love the tang Buffalo wing sauce adds to the flavors or feta cheese and ranch salad dressing.
—Tara Odegaard Omaha, NE

Prep: 35 min. • **Cook:** 3 hours
Makes: 16 servings

1½ pounds boneless skinless chicken breasts
2 tablespoons ranch salad dressing mix
½ cup Buffalo wing sauce
2 tablespoons butter
16 egg roll wrappers
⅓ cup crumbled feta cheese
⅓ cup shredded part-skim mozzarella cheese
Ranch salad dressing, optional

1. In a 3-qt. slow cooker, combine chicken, dressing mix and wing sauce. Cook, covered, on low until chicken is tender, 3-4 hours.
2. To serve, preheat oven to 425°. Shred chicken with two forks; stir in butter.
3. With one corner of an egg roll wrapper facing you, place 3 tablespoons chicken mixture just below center of wrapper; top with 1 teaspoon each feta and mozzarella cheeses. (Cover the remaining wrappers with a damp paper towel until ready to use.) Fold bottom corner over filling; moisten remaining wrapper edges with water. Fold side corners toward center over filling; roll up tightly, pressing at the tip to seal. Place on parchment paper-lined baking sheets, seam side down. Repeat.
4. Bake until golden brown, 15-20 minutes. Let egg rolls stand 5 minutes before serving.

SLOW COOKER SPINACH ARTICHOKE DIP

Here's a creamy, delicious and easy appetizer that's perfect for special occasions. It is really good served with Asiago cheese bread for dipping.
—Diane Morrison Bradford, PA

Prep: 10 min. • **Cook:** 2 hours
Makes: 12 servings (¼ cup each)

1 can (14 ounces) water-packed artichoke hearts, drained and chopped
1 cup fresh baby spinach, chopped
½ cup sour cream
½ cup mayonnaise
½ cup shredded part-skim mozzarella cheese
½ cup shredded Parmesan cheese
⅓ cup chopped red onion
¼ teaspoon garlic powder
Whole wheat baguette slices, chunks of rainbow carrots and celery

1. Place the first eight ingredients in a 1½-qt. slow cooker; stir to combine. Cook, covered, on low 2 to 2½ hours or until heated through.
2. Stir to blend. Serve with whole wheat baguette slices and chunks of rainbow carrots and celery.

★★★★★ **READER REVIEW**

"I made this for a group of friends and they said it was the best artichoke dip they've ever had! And then they asked for the recipe...delicious!"
COUNTRY-GIRL99 TASTEOFHOME.COM

SPICY CHICKEN EGG ROLLS

SWEET-AND-SOUR CHICKEN WINGS

SWEET-AND-SOUR CHICKEN WINGS

These wings are a fun appetizer for gatherings. I also like to serve them over rice as a main dish. Any way you do it, they'll be a hit!

—June Eberhardt Marysville, CA

Prep: 15 min. • **Cook:** 3 hours
Makes: 32 appetizers

- **1 cup sugar**
- **1 cup cider vinegar**
- **½ cup ketchup**
- **2 tablespoons reduced-sodium soy sauce**
- **1 teaspoon chicken bouillon granules**
- **16 chicken wings**
- **3 tablespoons cornstarch**
- **½ cup cold water**

1. In a small saucepan, combine the first five ingredients. Bring to a boil; cook and stir until sugar is dissolved.
2. Meanwhile, using a sharp knife, cut through the two wing joints; discard wing tips. Transfer the wings to a 5-qt. slow cooker; add sugar mixture. Cover and cook on low until chicken juices run clear, 3 to 3½ hours.
3. Transfer wings to a serving dish; keep warm. Skim fat from cooking juices; transfer to a small saucepan. Bring liquid to a boil. Combine cornstarch and water until smooth. Gradually stir into pan. Bring to a boil; cook and stir until thickened, about 2 minutes. Spoon over chicken. Serve with a slotted spoon.

Note: Uncooked chicken wing sections (wingettes) may be substituted for whole chicken wings.

★★★★★ **READER REVIEW**

"Another awesome recipe! Doubled it and served to a group, and they loved them! Will add this to my list of 'what to make for a party' foods!"

WENDYS1989 TASTEOFHOME.COM

CHOCOLATY PEANUT CLUSTERS

I turn to my slow cooker to prepare these yummy chocolate bites. Making candies couldn't be any easier!
—**Pam Posey** Waterloo, SC

Prep: 25 min. • **Cook:** 2 hours + standing
Makes: 6½ pounds

- 1 jar (16 ounces) salted dry roasted peanuts
- 1 jar (16 ounces) unsalted dry roasted peanuts
- 1 package (11½ ounces) milk chocolate chips
- 1 package (10 ounces) peanut butter chips
- 3 packages (10 to 12 ounces each) white baking chips
- 2 packages (10 ounces each) 60% cacao bittersweet chocolate baking chips

1. In a 6-qt. slow cooker, combine peanuts. Layer with the remaining ingredients in order given (do not stir). Cover and cook on low for 2-2½ hours or until chips are melted, stirring halfway through cooking.
2. Stir to combine. Drop by tablespoonfuls onto waxed paper. Refrigerate until set. Store in an airtight container at room temperature.

CHOCOLATY PEANUT CLUSTERS

JALAPENO SPINACH DIP

Everyone loves spinach dip, and this version is as easy as it is delicious. Just mix the ingredients together in the slow cooker for a savory and creamy appetizer.
—**Michaela Debelius** Waddell, AZ

Prep: 10 min. • **Cook:** 2 hours
Makes: 16 servings (¼ cup each)

- 2 packages (10 ounces each) frozen chopped spinach, thawed and squeezed dry
- 2 packages (8 ounces each) cream cheese, softened
- 1 cup grated Parmesan cheese
- 1 cup half-and-half cream
- ½ cup finely chopped onion
- ¼ cup chopped seeded jalapeno peppers
- 2 teaspoons Worcestershire sauce
- 2 teaspoons hot pepper sauce
- 1 teaspoon garlic powder
- 1 teaspoon dill weed
- Tortilla chips

In a 1½-qt. slow cooker, combine the first 10 ingredients. Cover and cook on low for 2-3 hours or until heated through. Serve with chips.

Note: Wear disposable gloves when cutting hot peppers; the oils can burn skin. Avoid touching your face.

MARINATED CHICKEN WINGS

I've made these nicely flavored chicken wings many times for get-togethers. They're so moist and tender. I always get lots of compliments and requests for the no-fuss recipe.

—Janie Botting Sultan, WA

Prep: 5 min. + marinating • **Cook:** 3 hours
Makes: 20 servings

- **20 chicken wings (about 4 pounds)**
- **1 cup reduced-sodium soy sauce**
- **¼ cup white wine or reduced-sodium chicken broth**
- **¼ cup canola oil**
- **3 tablespoons sugar**
- **2 garlic cloves, minced**
- **1 teaspoon ground ginger**

1. Cut chicken wings into three sections; discard wing tips. Place in a large resealable plastic bag. In a small bowl, whisk remaining ingredients until blended. Add to chicken; seal bag and turn to coat. Refrigerate overnight.
2. Transfer chicken and marinade to a 5-qt. slow cooker. Cook, covered, on low 3-4 hours or until chicken is tender. Using tongs, remove wings to a serving plate.

Note: To brown wings before serving, preheat broiler. Using tongs, remove wings from slow cooker to a foil-lined baking sheet. Broil 3-4 in. from heat 3-5 minutes or until lightly browned.

DID YOU KNOW?

The easiest way to cut a chicken wing into sections is to place the wing on a cutting board. With a sharp knife, cut between the joint at the top of the tip end. Discard the tip. Cut the remaining wing between the joints. Proceed with recipe as directed.

GARLIC SWISS FONDUE

I've been making this recipe for years—everyone flips over the wonderful flavors. When cooled, this cheesy appetizer is also fantastic as a cracker spread.

—Cleo Gonske Redding, CA

Prep: 10 min. • **Cook:** 2 hours
Makes: 3 cups

- **4 cups shredded Swiss cheese**
- **1 can (10¾ ounces) condensed cheddar cheese soup, undiluted**
- **2 tablespoons sherry or chicken broth**
- **1 tablespoon Dijon mustard**
- **2 garlic cloves, minced**
- **2 teaspoons hot pepper sauce**
- **Cubed French bread baguette, sliced apples and seedless red grapes**

In a 1½-qt. slow cooker, mix the first six ingredients. Cook, covered, on low 2 to 2½ hours or until cheese is melted, stirring every 30 minutes. Serve warm with bread cubes and fruit.

SWEET & SPICY PEANUTS

With a caramel-like coating, these crunchy peanuts have a touch of heat from the hot sauce. They make a tasty snack any time of day.

***—Taste of Home* Test Kitchen**

Prep: 10 min. • **Cook:** 1½ hours + cooling
Makes: 4 cups

- **3 cups salted peanuts**
- **½ cup sugar**
- **⅓ cup packed brown sugar**
- **2 tablespoons hot water**
- **2 tablespoons butter, melted**
- **1 tablespoon Sriracha Asian hot chili sauce or hot pepper sauce**
- **1 teaspoon chili powder**

1. Place peanuts in a greased 1½-qt. slow cooker. In a small bowl, combine the sugars, water, butter, hot sauce and chili powder. Pour over peanuts. Cover and cook on high for 1½ hours, stirring once.
2. Spread on waxed paper to cool. Store in an airtight container.

GARLIC SWISS FONDUE

SOUTHWESTERN NACHOS

SOUTHWESTERN NACHOS

Guests will go crazy when you serve this cheesy nacho casserole with tender chunks of pork. The tortilla chips are conveniently baked right in the dish, and since it makes two pans, you won't have to worry about refilling anything!
—**Kelly Byler** Goshen, IN

Prep: 40 min. • **Cook:** 7¼ hours
Makes: 30 servings

- **2 boneless whole pork loin roasts (3½ pounds each)**
- **1 cup unsweetened apple juice**
- **6 garlic cloves, minced**
- **1 teaspoon salt**
- **1 teaspoon liquid smoke, optional**
- **2½ cups barbecue sauce**
- **⅓ cup packed brown sugar**
- **2 tablespoons honey**
- **1 package (16 ounces) tortilla chips**
- **1½ cups frozen corn**
- **1 can (15 ounces) black beans, rinsed and drained**
- **1 medium tomato, seeded and chopped**
- **1 medium red onion, chopped**
- **⅓ cup minced fresh cilantro**
- **1 jalapeno pepper, seeded and chopped**
- **2 teaspoons lime juice**
- **1 package (16 ounces) process cheese (Velveeta), cubed**
- **¼ cup 2% milk**

1. Cut each roast in half; place in two 5-qt. slow cookers. Combine the apple juice, garlic, salt and, if desired, liquid smoke; pour over meat. Cover and cook on low 7-8 hours or until tender.
2. Preheat oven to 375°. Shred pork with two forks; place in a very large bowl. Stir in barbecue sauce, brown sugar and honey. Divide tortilla chips between two greased 13x9-in. baking dishes; top with pork mixture. Combine corn, beans, tomato, onion, cilantro, jalapeno and lime juice; spoon over pork mixture. Bake, uncovered, 15-20 minutes or until the mixture is heated through.
3. Meanwhile, in a small saucepan, melt cheese with milk. Drizzle cheese sauce over nachos.

Note: Wear disposable gloves when cutting hot peppers; the oils can burn skin. Avoid touching your face.

BARBECUE SAUSAGE BITES

This irresistible appetizer pairs tangy pineapple with sweet barbecue sauce and three kinds of sausage. It'll tide over even the biggest appetites until dinner.
—**Rebekah Randolph** Greer, SC

Prep: 10 min. • **Cook:** 2½ hours
Makes: 14 servings

- **1 package (16 ounces) miniature smoked sausages**
- **¾ pound fully cooked bratwurst links, cut into ½-inch slices**
- **¾ pound smoked kielbasa or Polish sausage, cut into ½-inch slices**
- **1 bottle (18 ounces) barbecue sauce**
- **⅔ cup orange marmalade**
- **½ teaspoon ground mustard**
- **⅛ teaspoon ground allspice**
- **1 can (20 ounces) pineapple chunks, drained**

1. In a 3-qt. slow cooker, combine the sausages. In a small bowl, whisk the barbecue sauce, marmalade, mustard and allspice. Pour over sausage mixture; stir to coat.
2. Cover and cook on high for 2½ to 3 hours or until heated through. Stir in pineapple. Serve with toothpicks.

SLOW-COOKED
BIG BREAKFAST

BREAKFAST & BRUNCH

Rise and shine! Kick off summer days with 18 eye-opening recipes emphasizing flavor and convenience. No one will ever guess these dishes came from a slow cooker.

SLOW-COOKED BIG BREAKFAST

We make this during holidays or on mornings when we know we're going to have a busy day. You can set this to cook overnight on low for an early breakfast, or for three hours on high for a leisurely brunch.

—Delisha Paris Elizabeth Cty, NC

Prep: 30 min. • **Cook:** 3 hours
Makes: 12 servings

- **1 pound bulk pork sausage**
- **2 pounds potatoes (about 4 medium), peeled and cut into ½-in. cubes**
- **¼ cup water**
- **1 large onion, finely chopped**
- **1 medium sweet red pepper, chopped**
- **2 cups fresh spinach**
- **1 cup chopped fresh mushrooms**
- **1 pound cubed deli ham**
- **1 cup shredded cheddar cheese**
- **12 large eggs**
- **½ cup 2% milk**
- **1 teaspoon garlic powder**
- **1 teaspoon pepper**
- **½ teaspoon salt**

1. In a large skillet, cook and crumble sausage over medium heat until no longer pink, 5-7 minutes; drain.
2. Meanwhile, place potatoes and water in a large microwave-safe dish. Microwave, covered, on high until potatoes are tender, 6 minutes, stirring halfway. Drain and add to sausage.
3. Stir in onion, sweet red pepper, spinach mushrooms, ham and cheese. Transfer to a greased 6-qt. slow cooker.
4. Whisk together remaining ingredients until blended; pour over sausage mixture. Cook, covered, on low until eggs are set, 3-4 hours. Let stand, uncovered, 10 minutes before serving.

EGG & BROCCOLI CASSEROLE

For years, I've prepared this hearty casserole for brunches and potlucks. It's an unusual recipe for the slow cooker, but wherever I serve it, folks always welcome it and go back for seconds.

—Janet Sliter Kennewick, WA

Prep: 10 min. • **Cook:** 3½ hours
Makes: 6 servings

- **3 cups (24 ounces) 4% cottage cheese**
- **3 cups frozen chopped broccoli, thawed and drained**
- **2 cups shredded cheddar cheese**
- **6 large eggs, lightly beaten**
- **⅓ cup all-purpose flour**
- **¼ cup butter, melted**
- **3 tablespoons finely chopped onion**
- **½ teaspoon salt**
- **Additional shredded cheddar cheese, optional**

1. In a large bowl, combine the first eight ingredients. Pour into a greased 3-qt. slow cooker. Cover and cook on high for 1 hour. Stir.
2. Reduce heat to low; cover and cook for 2½ to 3 hours longer or until a thermometer reads 160°. Sprinkle with cheese if desired.

★★★★★ **READER REVIEW**

"Love to serve it for brunch. Just put everything in the slow cooker and you don't have to worry about it."

SLYE10001000 TASTEOFHOME.COM

DENVER OMELET
FRITTATA

DENVER OMELET FRITTATA

This frittata has the classic ingredients of a Denver omelet—peppers, onion and ham—along with potatoes to make it extra hearty. It's the perfect brunch dish to serve company after church or another early summer outing.

—Connie Eaton Pittsburgh, PA

Prep: 25 min. • **Cook:** 3 hours
Makes: 6 servings

- **1 cup water**
- **1 tablespoon olive oil**
- **1 medium Yukon Gold potato, peeled and sliced**
- **1 small onion, thinly sliced**
- **12 large eggs**
- **1 teaspoon hot pepper sauce**
- **½ teaspoon salt**
- **¼ teaspoon pepper**
- **½ pound deli ham, chopped**
- **½ cup chopped sweet green pepper**
- **1 cup shredded cheddar cheese, divided**

1. Layer two 24-in. pieces of aluminum foil; starting with a long side, fold foil to create a 1-in.-wide strip. Shape strip into a coil to make a rack for bottom of a 6-qt. oval slow cooker. Add water to slow cooker; set foil rack in water.
2. In a large skillet, heat oil over medium-high heat. Add potato and onion; cook and stir 4-6 minutes or until potato is lightly browned. Transfer to a greased 1½-qt. baking dish (dish must fit in the slow cooker).
3. In a large bowl, whisk eggs, pepper sauce, salt and pepper; stir in ham, green pepper and ½ cup cheese. Pour over potato mixture. Top with the remaining cheese. Place dish on foil rack.
4. Cook, covered, on low 3-4 hours or until eggs are set and a knife inserted in the center comes out clean.

HASH BROWN EGG BRUNCH

HASH BROWN EGG BRUNCH

Slow cookers aren't just for making dinner. I make this often if we're having company overnight. With just a little planning and no trouble, I can prep it the night before and have a lovely breakfast.

—Barb Keith Eau Claire, WI

Prep: 20 min. • **Cook:** 4 hours
Makes: 10 servings

- **1 package (30 ounces) frozen shredded hash brown potatoes, thawed**
- **1 pound bacon strips, cooked and crumbled**
- **1 medium onion, chopped**
- **1 medium green pepper, chopped**
- **1½ cups shredded cheddar cheese**
- **12 large eggs**
- **1 cup 2% milk**
- **½ teaspoon salt**
- **½ teaspoon pepper**

1. In a greased 5-qt. slow cooker, layer a third of each of the following: potatoes, bacon, onion, green pepper and cheese. Repeat layers twice. In a large bowl, whisk eggs, milk, salt and pepper; pour over the layers.
2. Cook, covered, on high 30 minutes. Reduce heat to low; cook, covered, until a thermometer reads160°, 3½ to 4 hours.

Farmer's Country Breakfast: Substitute ¾ pound bulk pork sausage, cooked and drained, for the bacon. Omit green pepper. Whisk ¼ cup minced fresh parsley into egg mixture. Cook as directed.

SPAM & Eggs Brunch: Substitute 2 cans (12 ounces each) SPAM luncheon meat, chopped, for the bacon. Whisk 2 minced garlic cloves into egg mixture. Cook as directed.

ONION-GARLIC HASH BROWNS

Quick to assemble, these slow-cooked hash browns are one of my go-to sides. Stir in hot sauce if you like a bit of heat. I top my finished dish with a sprinkling of shredded cheddar cheese.

—**Cindi Boger** Ardmore, AL

Prep: 20 min. • **Cook:** 3 hours
Makes: 12 servings (½ cup each)

- **¼ cup butter, cubed**
- **1 tablespoon olive oil**
- **1 large red onion, chopped**
- **1 small sweet red pepper, chopped**
- **1 small green pepper, chopped**
- **4 garlic cloves, minced**
- **1 package (30 ounces) frozen shredded hash brown potatoes**
- **½ teaspoon salt**
- **½ teaspoon pepper**
- **3 drops hot pepper sauce, optional**
- **2 teaspoons minced fresh parsley**

1. In a large skillet, heat butter and oil over medium heat. Add the onion and peppers. Cook and stir until crisp-tender. Add garlic; cook 1 minute longer. Stir in hash browns, salt, pepper and, if desired, pepper sauce.
2. Transfer to a 5-qt. slow cooker coated with cooking spray. Cook, covered, 3-4 hours or until heated through. Sprinkle with parsley just before serving.

ONION-GARLIC HASH BROWNS

SLOW COOKER HAM & EGGS

This recipe is great anytime of the year, but I love to make it for Easter. Start it in the morning before church and when you return, there's a wonderful dish ready for your family. I like to serve this alongside hash browns potatoes cooked up crisp in the frying pan.

—**Andrea Schaak** Jordan, MN

Prep: 15 min. • **Cook:** 3 hours
Makes: 6 servings

- **6 large eggs**
- **1 cup biscuit/baking mix**
- **⅔ cup 2% milk**
- **⅓ cup sour cream**
- **2 tablespoons minced fresh parsley**
- **2 garlic cloves, minced**
- **½ teaspoon salt**
- **½ teaspoon pepper**
- **1 cup cubed fully cooked ham**
- **1 cup shredded Swiss cheese**
- **1 small onion, finely chopped**
- **⅓ cup shredded Parmesan cheese**

1. In a large bowl, whisk the first eight ingredients until blended; stir in remaining ingredients. Pour into a greased 3- or 4-qt. slow cooker.
2. Cook, covered, on low 3-4 hours or until eggs are set. Cut into wedges.

QUINOA GRANOLA

I feed this healthy and tasty snack to my kids often. They love it!
—Cindy Reams Philipsburg, PA

Prep: 5 min. • **Cook:** 1 hour + cooling
Makes: 6 cups

- **¼ cup honey**
- **2 tablespoons coconut or canola oil**
- **1 teaspoon ground cinnamon**
- **3 cups old-fashioned oats**
- **1 cup uncooked quinoa**
- **1 cup sweetened shredded coconut**
- **1 cup chopped mixed dried fruit**
- **1 cup chopped pecans**

1. In a 3- or 4-qt. slow cooker, combine honey, oil and cinnamon. Gradually stir in oats and quinoa until well blended. Cook, covered, on high 1 to 1½ hours, stirring well every 20 minutes.

2. Stir in coconut, dried fruit and pecans. Spread evenly on waxed paper or baking sheets; cool completely. Store granola in airtight containers.

OVERNIGHT VEGETABLE & EGG BREAKFAST

My overnight eggs and veggies make a hearty breakfast for those who have to rush out the door. I use sliced potatoes, but frozen potatoes work, too.
—Kimberly Clark-Thiry Anchor Point, AK

Prep: 15 min. • **Cook:** 7 hours
Makes: 8 servings

- **4 pounds potatoes, peeled and thinly sliced (about 8 cups)**
- **1 medium green pepper, finely chopped**
- **1 package (10 ounces) frozen chopped spinach, thawed and squeezed dry**
- **1 cup sliced fresh mushrooms**
- **1 medium onion, finely chopped**
- **8 large eggs**
- **1 cup water**
- **1 cup 2% milk**
- **1¼ teaspoons salt**
- **¼ teaspoon pepper**
- **2 cups shredded cheddar cheese**

In a greased 6-qt. slow cooker, layer the first five ingredients. In a large bowl, whisk the next five ingredients; pour over top. Sprinkle with cheese. Cook, covered, on low until potatoes are tender and eggs are set, 7-9 hours.

SMOKY HASH BROWN CASSEROLE

(5) INGREDIENTS

SMOKY HASH BROWN CASSEROLE

Making this delicious, savory casserole in the slow cooker saves oven space, but you can bake it in the oven if you prefer. Just see the bake option below.
—Susan Hein Burlington, WI

Prep: 10 min. • **Cook:** 3½ hours
Makes: 6 servings

- **1 teaspoon butter**
- **1 package (28 ounces) frozen O'Brien potatoes, thawed**
- **1 can (10¾ ounces) condensed cream of chicken soup, undiluted**
- **4 ounces smoked cheddar cheese, shredded**
- **½ teaspoon pepper**
- **¼ teaspoon salt**

Grease a 3-qt. slow cooker with butter. Combine potatoes, soup, cheese, pepper and salt. Transfer to prepared slow cooker. Cook, covered, on low until potatoes are tender, 3½ to 4½ hours.
Bake option: Preheat the oven to 350°. Place potato mixture in a greased 13x9-in. baking dish. Bake, uncovered, until potatoes are tender, 45-55 minutes.

TEST KITCHEN TIP

If you forgot to thaw the potatoes for the Smoky Hash Brown Casserole, don't worry! Simply put the spuds in a colander and rinse with cold water until thawed. Next, give them a twirl in a salad spinner to remove the excess water. Then you're all set to prepare the recipe as directed.

VIENNESE COFFEE

(5) INGREDIENTS

VIENNESE COFFEE

This isn't your regular cup of joe! I dress it up with chocolate, whipped cream and more, making it a drink to savor.
—Sharon Delaney-Chronis
South Milwaukee, WI

Prep: 10 min. • **Cook:** 3 hours
Makes: 4 servings

- **3 cups strong brewed coffee**
- **3 tablespoons chocolate syrup**
- **1 teaspoon sugar**
- **⅓ cup heavy whipping cream**
- **¼ cup creme de cacao or Irish cream liqueur**
- **Whipped cream and chocolate curls, optional**

1. In a 1½-qt. slow cooker, combine the coffee, chocolate syrup and sugar. Cover and cook on low for 2½ hours.
2. Stir in heavy cream and creme de cacao. Cover and cook 30 minutes longer or until heated through.
3. Ladle coffee into mugs. Garnish with whipped cream and the chocolate curls if desired.

HOT FRUIT SALAD

If you're looking for something easy to round out a brunch, try this spiced fruit salad. With its pretty color, it's a perfect way to start the day or round out any special menu.
—Barb Vande Voort New Sharon, IA

Prep: 10 min. • **Cook:** 3 hours
Makes: 16 servings (¾ cup each)

- **1 jar (25 ounces) unsweetened applesauce**
- **1 can (21 ounces) cherry pie filling**
- **1 can (20 ounces) unsweetened pineapple chunks, undrained**
- **1 can (15 ounces) sliced peaches in juice, undrained**
- **1 can (15 ounces) reduced-sugar apricot halves, undrained**
- **1 can (15 ounces) mandarin oranges, undrained**
- **¼ cup packed brown sugar**
- **1 teaspoon ground cinnamon**

Combine first six ingredients in a 5-qt. slow cooker. Mix brown sugar and cinnamon; sprinkle over fruit mixture. Cook, covered, on low until heated through, 3-4 hours.

CINNAMON BLUEBERRY FRENCH TOAST

Prep this in the afternoon and let it chill in the fridge. I can get up early, put it all into the slow cooker and soon breakfast is done! All it takes is a little bit of planning. Swap out the French bread for whole wheat if you'd like to add a bit of fiber.
—**Angela Lively** Conroe, TX

Prep: 15 min. • **Cook:** 3 hours
Makes: 6 servings

- **3 large eggs**
- **2 cups 2% milk**
- **¼ cup sugar**
- **1 teaspoon ground cinnamon**
- **1 teaspoon vanilla extract**
- **¼ teaspoon salt**
- **9 cups cubed French bread (about 9 ounces)**
- **1 cup fresh or frozen blueberries, thawed**
- **Maple syrup**

1. Whisk together first six ingredients. Layer half of the bread in a greased 5-qt. slow cooker; top with ½ cup blueberries and half of the milk mixture. Repeat layers. Refrigerate, covered, 4 hours or overnight.
2. Cook, covered, on low until a knife inserted in the center comes out clean, 3-4 hours. Serve warm with syrup.

CINNAMON BLUEBERRY FRENCH TOAST

SWEET KAHLUA COFFEE

Want to perk up your java? With Kahlua, creme de cacao and a dollop of whipped cream, this chocolaty coffee makes the perfect sipper for bunch or an after-dinner delight. I love that it comes together on its own in the slow cooker.
—**Ruth Gruchow** Yorba Linda, CA

Prep: 10 min. • **Cook:** 3 hours
Makes: 8 servings (2¼ quarts)

- **2 quarts hot water**
- **½ cup Kahlua (coffee liqueur)**
- **¼ cup creme de cacao**
- **3 tablespoons instant coffee granules**
- **2 cups heavy whipping cream**
- **¼ cup sugar**
- **1 teaspoon vanilla extract**
- **2 tablespoons grated semisweet chocolate**

1. In a 4-qt. slow cooker, mix water, Kahlua, creme de cacao and coffee granules. Cook, covered, on low 3-4 hours or until heated through.
2. In a large bowl, beat cream until it begins to thicken. Add sugar and vanilla; beat until soft peaks form. Serve warm coffee with whipped cream topped with grated chocolate.

HAM & CHEDDAR BREAKFAST CASSEROLE

This easy, cheesy casserole is my go-to recipe for action-packed mornings. It's made several appearances at potlucks, special celebrations and even at my daughter's college apartment to feed her hungry roommates.

—**Patty Bernhard** Greenville, OH

Prep: 20 min. + chilling
Cook: 4 hours + standing
Makes: 12 servings

12 large eggs
1 cup 2% milk
1 teaspoon salt
½ teaspoon pepper
1 package (30 ounces) frozen shredded hash brown potatoes, thawed
2 cups cubed fully cooked ham (about 1 pound)
1 medium onion, chopped
4 cups shredded cheddar cheese

1. Whisk together first four ingredients. Place a third of the potatoes in a greased 5- or 6-qt. slow cooker; layer with a third of each of the following: ham, onion and cheese. Repeat layers twice. Pour egg mixture over top. Refrigerate, covered, overnight.

2. Cook, covered, on low until set and edges begin to brown, 4-5 hours. Turn off slow cooker. Remove insert; let stand, uncovered, 30 minutes before serving.

DID YOU KNOW?

Shredding a block of cheese yourself almost always leads to better cooking results than you'll get with packaged shredded cheese. Read the label: the contents include starch, cellulose and antimold agents. They may keep the strands from sticking together. But they can also interfere with flavor and melting. So go ahead and grate for great taste and texture—and lower cost!

CHILI & CHEESE CRUSTLESS QUICHE

This hearty Tex-Mex dish is a standout at breakfast or any time of the day. For dinner, I simply add a salad.

—Gail Watkins Norwalk, CA

Prep: 15 min. • **Cook:** 3 hours + standing
Makes: 6 servings

- **3 corn tortillas (6 inches)**
- **2 cans (4 ounces each) whole green chilies**
- **1 can (15 ounces) chili con carne**
- **1½ cups shredded cheddar cheese, divided**
- **4 large eggs**
- **1½ cups 2% milk**
- **1 cup biscuit/baking mix**
- **¼ teaspoon salt**
- **¼ teaspoon pepper**
- **1 teaspoon hot pepper sauce, optional**
- **1 can (4 ounces) chopped green chilies**
- **2 medium tomatoes, sliced**
- **Sour cream, optional**

1. In a greased 4- or 5-qt. slow cooker, layer tortillas, whole green chilies, chili con carne and 1 cup cheese.
2. In a small bowl, whisk eggs, milk, biscuit mix, salt, pepper and, if desired, pepper sauce until blended; pour into slow cooker. Top with chopped green chilies and tomatoes.
3. Cook, covered, on low 3-4 hours or until a thermometer reads 160°, sprinkling with remaining cheese during the last 30 minutes of cooking. Turn off slow cooker; remove insert. Let stand 15 minutes before serving. If desired, top with sour cream.

TEST KITCHEN TIP

Don't lift the lid unless the recipe tells you to! Keep the cover shut on your slow cooker or you risk the chance of increasing cook time.

SLOW COOKER CHORIZO BREAKFAST CASSEROLE

SLOW COOKER CHORIZO BREAKFAST CASSEROLE

My kids ask for this slow-cooked casserole all the time. I've served it with white country gravy or salsa— it's delightful either way.

—Cindy Pruitt Grove, OK

Prep: 25 min. • **Cook:** 4 hours + standing
Makes: 8 servings

- **1 pound fresh chorizo or bulk spicy pork sausage**
- **1 medium onion, chopped**
- **1 medium sweet red pepper, chopped**
- **2 jalapeno peppers, seeded and chopped**
- **1 package (30 ounces) frozen shredded hash brown potatoes, thawed**
- **1½ cups shredded Mexican cheese blend**
- **12 large eggs**
- **1 cup 2% milk**
- **½ teaspoon pepper**

1. In a large skillet, cook chorizo, onion, red pepper and jalapenos over medium heat 7-8 minutes or until cooked through and vegetables are tender, breaking chorizo into crumbles; drain. Cool slightly.
2. In a greased 5-qt. slow cooker, layer a third of the potatoes, chorizo mixture and cheese. Repeat layers twice. In a large bowl, whisk eggs, milk and pepper until blended; pour over top.
3. Cook, covered, on low 4-4½ hours or until eggs are set and a thermometer reads 160°. Uncover and let stand 10 minutes before serving.

Note: Wear disposable gloves when cutting hot peppers; the oils can burn skin. Avoid touching your face.

SLOW-COOKED BLUEBERRY FRENCH TOAST

Your slow cooker can be your best friend on a busy morning. Just get this recipe going, run some errands and come back to the aroma of French toast ready to eat.
—Elizabeth Lorenz Peru, IN

Prep: 30 min. + chilling • **Cook:** 3 hours
Makes: 12 servings (2 cups syrup)

- **8 large eggs**
- **½ cup plain yogurt**
- **⅓ cup sour cream**
- **1 teaspoon vanilla extract**
- **½ teaspoon ground cinnamon**
- **1 cup 2% milk**
- **⅓ cup maple syrup**
- **1 loaf (1 pound) French bread, cubed**
- **1½ cups fresh or frozen blueberries**
- **12 ounces cream cheese, cubed**

BLUEBERRY SYRUP

- **1 cup sugar**
- **2 tablespoons cornstarch**
- **1 cup cold water**
- **¾ cup fresh or frozen blueberries, divided**
- **1 tablespoon butter**
- **1 tablespoon lemon juice**

1. In a large bowl, whisk eggs, yogurt, sour cream, vanilla and cinnamon. Gradually whisk in milk and maple syrup until blended.
2. Place half of the bread in a greased 5- or 6-qt. slow cooker; layer with half of the blueberries, cream cheese and egg mixture. Repeat the layers. Refrigerate, covered, overnight.
3. Remove from refrigerator 30 minutes before cooking. Cook, covered, on low 3-4 hours or until a knife inserted in the center comes out clean.
4. For syrup, in a small saucepan, mix sugar and cornstarch; stir in water until smooth. Stir in ¼ cup blueberries. Bring to a boil; cook and stir until berries pop, about 3 minutes. Remove from heat; stir in butter, lemon juice and remaining berries. Serve warm with French toast.

SLOW-COOKED BLUEBERRY FRENCH TOAST

TROPICAL TEA

Try brewing a batch of this fragrant, flavorful tea in a slow cooker for your next family gathering. I just adore the refreshing flavors of pineapple and orange sweetened with a hint of honey.
—Irene Helen Zundel Carmichaels, PA

Prep: 15 min. • **Cook:** 2 hours
Makes: 10 servings (2½ quarts)

- **6 cups boiling water**
- **6 individual tea bags**
- **1½ cups orange juice**
- **1½ cups unsweetened pineapple juice**
- **⅓ cup sugar**
- **1 medium navel orange, halved and sliced**
- **2 tablespoons honey**
- **Pineapple and orange wedges, optional**

1. In a 5-qt. slow cooker, combine boiling water and tea bags. Cover and let stand for 5 minutes. Discard tea bags. Stir in the remaining ingredients.
2. Cover and cook on low for 2-4 hours or until heated through. If desired, serve with pineapple and orange wedges. Serve the tea warm.

SOUPS & SANDWICHES

When serving speed is key, turn to this dynamic duo and simmer up a winning combination tonight! It's a pairing that satisfies all appetites.

SLOW COOKER ITALIAN BEEF SANDWICHES

I have fond memories of my mother in the kitchen preparing her amazing beef dip sandwiches. They always made our house smell like an Old World Italian restaurant. And as good as the aroma was, somehow the taste was even better! Set out a jar of giardiniera for dressing up the top.
—Kira Vosk Milwaukee, WI

Prep: 1 hour • **Cook:** 7 hours
Makes: 12 servings

- **4 tablespoons olive oil, divided**
- **1 boneless beef chuck eye or other boneless beef chuck roast (4 to 5 pounds)**
- **2¼ teaspoons salt, divided**
- **2¼ teaspoons pepper, divided**
- **2 small onions, coarsely chopped**
- **9 garlic cloves, chopped**
- **¾ cup dry red wine**
- **4 cups beef stock**
- **3 fresh thyme sprigs**
- **4 teaspoons Italian seasoning**
- **1½ teaspoons crushed red pepper flakes**
- **4 medium green peppers, cut into ½-inch strips**
- **1 teaspoon garlic powder**
- **12 crusty submarine buns or hoagie buns, split partway**
- **12 slices provolone or part-skim mozzarella cheese**
- **Giardiniera, optional**

1. In a 6-qt. stockpot, heat 3 tablespoons oil over medium-high heat; brown roast on all sides. Sprinkle with 2 teaspoons each salt and pepper. Transfer to a 6-qt. slow cooker.
2. Add onions to stockpot; cook and stir 2-3 minutes or until lightly browned. Add garlic; cook 30 seconds longer. Add wine; cook for 3-5 minutes, stirring to loosen browned bits from pan. Stir in the stock, thyme, Italian seasoning and pepper flakes; transfer to slow cooker. Cook, covered, on low 7-9 hours or until beef is tender.
3. About ½ hour before serving, preheat oven to 350°. Place the peppers in a 15x10x1-in. baking pan. Drizzle with remaining oil. Sprinkle with garlic powder and the remaining salt and pepper; toss to coat. Roast 15-20 minutes or until softened, stirring halfway.
4. Remove roast; cool slightly. Strain cooking juices into a small saucepan, reserving strained mixture and removing thyme stems. Skim fat from juices; heat through and keep warm. Coarsely shred beef with two forks; stir in reserved strained mixture. If desired, moisten beef with some of the cooking juices.
5. To serve, preheat broiler. Arrange buns on baking sheets, cut side up. Broil 3-4 inches from heat until lightly toasted. Remove from oven; top each bun with ⅔ cup beef mixture and 1 slice cheese. Broil until cheese is melted, about 30 seconds.
6. Top with peppers and, if desired, giardiniera. Serve with cooking juices for dipping.

SLOW COOKER ITALIAN BEEF SANDWICHES

SLOW COOKER PORK POZOLE

I often make a heartwarming stew with pork ribs and hominy. This is a fill-you-up recipe of lightly spiced comfort.
—Genie Gunn Asheville, NC

Prep: 10 min. • **Cook:** 3 hours
Makes: 6 servings

- **1 can (15½ ounces) hominy, rinsed and drained**
- **1 can (14½ ounces) diced tomatoes, undrained**
- **1 can (14½ ounces) diced tomatoes with mild green chilies, undrained**
- **1 can (10 ounces) green enchilada sauce**
- **2 medium carrots, finely chopped**
- **1 medium onion, finely chopped**
- **3 garlic cloves, minced**
- **2 teaspoons ground cumin**
- **¼ teaspoon salt**
- **1 pound boneless country-style pork ribs**
- **Lime wedges and minced fresh cilantro**
- **Corn tortillas, optional**

1. In a 3- or 4-qt. slow cooker, combine the first nine ingredients; add pork. Cook, covered, on low for 3-4 hours or until the pork is tender.
2. Remove pork from slow cooker. Cut pork into bite-sized pieces; return to slow cooker. Serve with the lime wedges and cilantro and, if desired, corn tortillas.

SAUSAGE & CHICKEN GUMBO

This recipe for the classic southern comfort food was the first thing I ever cooked for my girlfriend. It was simple to make but tasted gourmet. Lucky for me, it was love at first bite.

—**Kael Harvey** Brooklyn, NY

Prep: 35 min. • **Cook:** 6 hours
Makes: 6 servings

- ¼ **cup all-purpose flour**
- ¼ **cup canola oil**
- 4 **cups chicken broth, divided**
- 1 **package (14 ounces) smoked sausage, cut into ½-inch slices**
- 1 **cup frozen sliced okra, thawed**
- 1 **small green pepper, chopped**
- 1 **medium onion, chopped**
- 1 **celery rib, chopped**
- 3 **garlic cloves, minced**
- ½ **teaspoon pepper**
- ¼ **teaspoon salt**
- ¼ **teaspoon cayenne pepper**
- 2 **cups coarsely shredded cooked chicken**
- **Hot cooked rice**

1. In a heavy saucepan, mix flour and oil until smooth; cook and stir over medium heat until light brown, about 4 minutes. Reduce heat to medium-low; cook and stir until dark reddish brown, about 15 minutes (do not burn). Gradually stir in 3 cups broth; transfer to a 4- or 5-qt. slow cooker.

2. Stir in sausage, vegetables, garlic and seasonings. Cook, covered, on low until flavors are blended, 6-8 hours. Stir in chicken and the remaining broth; heat through. Serve with rice.

Freeze option: Freeze cooled soup in freezer containers. To use, partially thaw in refrigerator overnight. Heat through in a saucepan, stirring soup occasionally and adding a little broth if necessary.

TEST KITCHEN TIP
To lighten up this gumbo, use 7 oz. smoked turkey sausage, 3 cups chicken, reduced-sodium broth and nix the salt.

PB&J PORK SANDWICHES

I came up with this recipe for one of my daughters who loves peanut butter. The result has become a family favorite, and children and grown-ups alike request it for dinner often.

—Jill Cox Lincoln, NE

Prep: 15 min. • **Cook:** 6 hours
Makes: 6 servings

- **3 to 4 pounds boneless pork shoulder butt roast**
- **1 teaspoon salt**
- **½ teaspoon pepper**
- **1 can (14½ ounces) reduced-sodium chicken broth**
- **1 cup creamy peanut butter**
- **¾ cup apricot preserves**
- **¼ cup packed brown sugar**
- **¼ cup finely chopped onion**
- **¼ cup cider vinegar**
- **3 tablespoons Dijon mustard**
- **1 garlic clove, minced**
- **2 tablespoons butter, melted**
- **6 ciabatta rolls, split**
- **Coleslaw, optional**

1. Sprinkle roast with salt and pepper; transfer to a 5-qt. slow cooker. In a large bowl, whisk the broth, peanut butter, preserves, brown sugar, onion, vinegar, mustard and garlic; pour over meat. Cook, covered, on low for 6-8 hours or until meat is tender.
2. Preheat broiler. Remove roast; cool slightly. Shred pork with two forks. Return pork to the slow cooker; heat through. Brush butter over cut sides of rolls. Place rolls, buttered side up, on an ungreased baking sheet. Broil 3-4 in. from heat 30-60 seconds or until golden brown. Using a slotted spoon, set pork mixture onto roll bottoms; top with coleslaw if desired. Replace tops.

PB & J PORK SANDWICHES

COCONUT-LIME CHICKEN CURRY SOUP

I created this recipe to replicate the flavors of my favorite curry dish—slightly sweet with just the right amount of spicy heat. When served with a garnish of green onions and toasted coconut, the soup makes the perfect cold-weather meal.

—Lisa Renshaw Kansas City, MO

Prep: 15 min. • **Cook:** 4¼ hours
Makes: 8 servings (2½ quarts)

- **2 cans (13.66 ounces each) light coconut milk**
- **2 cans (4 ounces each) chopped green chilies**
- **8 green onions, sliced**
- **2 teaspoons grated lime peel**
- **½ cup lime juice**
- **¼ cup sweet chili sauce**
- **6 garlic cloves, minced**
- **4 teaspoons curry powder**
- **½ teaspoon salt**
- **2 pounds boneless skinless chicken thighs, cut into ½-inch pieces**
- **3 cups cooked basmati rice**
- **Minced fresh cilantro**

1. Place the first nine ingredients in a 4- or 5-qt. slow cooker; stir in chicken. Cook, covered, on low 4-5 hours or until chicken is tender.
2. Skim fat; stir in cooked rice. Cook, covered, on low 15-30 minutes or until heated through. Sprinkle individual servings with cilantro.

CHUCK ROAST SAMMIES

This hearty slow-cooked specialty is particularly irresistible during parties. The savory sandwiches are perfect while cozying up for sporting events, game nights or movies.

—**Catherine Cassidy** Milwaukee, WI

Prep: 30 min. • **Cook:** 7 hours
Makes: 18 servings

- **1 boneless beef chuck roast (4 to 5 pounds)**
- **4 teaspoons Montreal steak seasoning**
- **3 tablespoons butter**
- **1 medium onion, chopped**
- **2 celery ribs, chopped**
- **1 small carrot, finely chopped**
- **½ cup seeded and chopped pepperoncini**
- **½ cup fresh basil leaves, thinly sliced**
- **4 garlic cloves, minced**
- **2 cups beef broth**
- **1½ cups chili sauce**
- **1 bottle (12 ounces) beer**
- **3 tablespoons reduced-sodium soy sauce**
- **1 tablespoon dried rosemary, crushed**
- **1 bay leaf**
- **¼ teaspoon salt**
- **¼ teaspoon pepper**

ASSEMBLY

- **18 mini buns, split**
- **Additional chopped pepperoncini, sliced red onion, dill pickle slices and stone-ground mustard, optional**

1. Trim the roast; sprinkle with steak seasoning. Cut roast in half. In a large skillet, heat butter over medium heat; brown meat in batches. Transfer meat and drippings to a 6-qt. slow cooker. Add remaining ingredients. Cook, covered, on low 7-8 hours or until meat is tender.
2. Remove roast; cool slightly. Strain cooking juices, discarding vegetables and bay leaf; skim fat. Shred meat with two forks. Return meat and cooking juices to slow cooker; heat through.
3. Using tongs, place meat on bun bottoms. Serve with cooking juices for dipping and top as desired.

CHEESY HAM & CORN CHOWDER

CHEESY HAM & CORN CHOWDER

When the day calls for a warm bowl of chunky comforting soup, we haul out the slow cooker and whip up a big batch of this satisfying favorite.

—**Andrea Laidlaw** Shady Side, MD

Prep: 25 min. • **Cook:** 8½ hours
Makes: 12 servings (3¾ quarts)

- **1½ pounds potatoes (about 3 medium), peeled and cut into ½-inch cubes**
- **4 cups fresh or frozen corn, thawed (about 20 ounces)**
- **4 cups cubed deli ham**
- **2 small onions, chopped**
- **4 celery ribs, chopped**
- **4 garlic cloves, minced**
- **¼ teaspoon pepper**
- **3 cups chicken broth**
- **2 tablespoons cornstarch**
- **2 cups whole milk**
- **2 cups shredded sharp cheddar cheese**
- **1 cup sour cream**
- **3 tablespoons minced fresh parsley**

1. Place the first eight ingredients in a 6-qt. slow cooker. Cook, covered, on low 8-10 hours or until potatoes are tender.
2. In a small bowl, mix cornstarch and milk until smooth; stir into soup. Cook, covered, on high 20-30 minutes or until thickened, stirring occasionally. Stir in cheese, sour cream and parsley until cheese is melted.

SWEET & SOUR PORK WRAPS

We always make these wraps at our family's annual party, and everyone enjoys them. The cabbage and cilantro give them great texture and flavor.
—Andrew DeVito Hartford, CT

Prep: 15 min. • **Cook:** 6 hours
Makes: 8 servings (2 wraps each)

- **1 boneless pork shoulder butt roast (3 to 4 pounds)**
- **1 medium onion, chopped**
- **1 cup water**
- **1 cup sweet-and-sour sauce**
- **¼ cup sherry or chicken broth**
- **¼ cup reduced-sodium soy sauce**
- **1 envelope onion soup mix**
- **1 tablespoon minced fresh gingerroot**
- **3 garlic cloves, minced**
- **16 flour tortillas (6 inches), warmed**
- **4 cups shredded cabbage**
- **¼ cup minced fresh cilantro**

1. Place roast and onion in a 6-qt. slow cooker. In a small bowl, whisk water, sweet-and-sour sauce, sherry, soy sauce, soup mix, ginger and garlic until blended; pour over pork. Cook, covered, on low 6-8 hours or until meat is tender.
2. When cool enough to handle, shred pork with two forks. To serve, spoon about ⅓ cup pork mixture onto the center of each tortilla. Top with ¼ cup cabbage; sprinkle with cilantro. Fold bottom of tortilla over filling; fold both sides to close.

SWEET & SOUR PORK WRAPS

BBQ HAM SANDWICHES

Friends love these barbecue sandwiches and often ask me to make them. I double the crowd-pleaser recipe to serve the hoagies at potlucks.
—Dana Knox Butler, PA

Prep: 20 min. • **Cook:** 2 hours
Makes: 16 servings

- **3 cups ketchup**
- **¾ cup chopped onion**
- **¾ cup chopped green pepper**
- **¾ cup packed brown sugar**
- **½ cup lemon juice**
- **⅓ cup Worcestershire sauce**
- **1 tablespoon prepared mustard**
- **1¼ teaspoons ground allspice**
- **1½ teaspoons liquid smoke, optional**
- **3 pounds thinly sliced deli ham**
- **16 kaiser or ciabatta rolls, split**

1. In a large saucepan, combine the first eight ingredients; if desired, stir in liquid smoke. Bring to a boil over medium-high heat. Reduce heat; simmer, uncovered, for 5 minutes, stirring occasionally.
2. Place ham in a 5- or 6-qt. slow cooker. Add sauce; stir gently to combine. Cook, covered, on low 2-3 hours or until heated through. Serve on rolls.

CAROLINA-STYLE
VINEGAR BBQ CHICKEN

(5) INGREDIENTS

CAROLINA-STYLE VINEGAR BBQ CHICKEN

I live in Georgia but I appreciate the tangy, sweet and slightly spicy taste of Carolina vinegar chicken. I make my version in the slow cooker. When you walk in the door after being gone all day, the aroma will knock you off your feet!

—**Ramona Parris** Canton, GA

Prep: 10 min. • **Cook:** 4 hours
Makes: 6 servings

- **2 cups water**
- **1 cup white vinegar**
- **¼ cup sugar**
- **1 tablespoon reduced-sodium chicken base**
- **1 teaspoon crushed red pepper flakes**
- **¾ teaspoon salt**
- **1½ pounds boneless skinless chicken breasts**
- **6 whole wheat hamburger buns, split, optional**

1. In a small bowl, mix the first six ingredients. Place chicken in a 3-qt. slow cooker; add the vinegar mixture. Cook, covered, on low 4-5 hours or until chicken is tender.
2. Remove chicken; cool slightly. Reserve 1 cup cooking juices; discard remaining juices. Shred chicken with two forks. Return meat and reserved cooking juices to slow cooker; heat through. If desired, serve chicken mixture on buns.

Note: Look for chicken base near the broth and bouillon.

★★★★★ **READER REVIEW**

"A winner of a chicken dinner! I am not used to a vinegar-based BBQ, but this is absolutely delicious. The best part is that it's a dump-and-go recipe. The slow cooker makes it super simple. We'll be making this again soon!"

ALLISONO TASTEOFHOME.COM

CHICKEN FAJITA CHOWDER

CHICKEN FAJITA CHOWDER

This south-of-the-border entree is one of my favorite slow cooker recipes, and it's popular at family dinners and potlucks alike. We top ours with fresh avocado, shredded cheddar cheese and chili cheese corn chips.

—**Nancy Heishman** Las Vegas, NV

Prep: 20 min. • **Cook:** 4 hours
Makes: 10 servings (3½ quarts)

- **3 large tomatoes, chopped**
- **1 can (15 ounces) black beans, rinsed and drained**
- **6 ounces fully cooked Spanish chorizo links, sliced**
- **2 pounds boneless skinless chicken breasts, cut into 1-inch cubes**
- **1 envelope fajita seasoning mix**
- **1½ cups frozen corn, thawed**
- **1 medium sweet red pepper, chopped**
- **1 medium green pepper, chopped**
- **6 green onions, chopped**
- **¾ cup salsa**
- **½ cup chopped fresh cilantro**
- **2 cans (14½ ounces each) reduced-sodium chicken broth**
- **1 can (10¾ ounces) condensed nacho cheese soup, undiluted**
- **Cubed avocado and additional cilantro, optional**

1. Place first twelve ingredients in a 6-qt. slow cooker. Cook, covered, on low until chicken is tender, 4-5 hours.
2. Stir in cheese soup; heat through. If desired, top servings with avocado and additional cilantro.

Freeze option: Freeze cooled soup in freezer containers. To use, partially thaw in refrigerator overnight. Heat through in a saucepan, stirring occasionally.

BEER-BRAISED PULLED HAM

To jazz up leftover ham, I slow-cooked it with a beer sauce. Buns loaded with ham, pickles and mustard are irresistible.
—Ann Sheehy Lawrence, MA

Prep: 10 min. • **Cook:** 7 hours
Makes: 16 servings

2 bottles (12 ounces each) beer or nonalcoholic beer
¾ cup German or Dijon mustard, divided
½ teaspoon coarsely ground pepper
1 fully cooked bone-in ham (about 4 pounds)
4 fresh rosemary sprigs
16 pretzel hamburger buns, split
Dill pickle slices, optional

1. In a 5-qt. slow cooker, whisk together beer and ½ cup mustard. Stir in pepper. Add ham and rosemary. Cook, covered, on low until tender, 7-9 hours.
2. Remove ham; cool slightly. Discard rosemary sprigs. Skim fat. When ham is cool enough to handle, shred meat with two forks. Discard bone. Return to slow cooker; heat through.
3. Using tongs, place shredded ham on pretzel buns; top with remaining mustard and, if desired, dill pickle slices.

Freeze option: Freeze cooled ham mixture in freezer containers. To use, partially thaw in refrigerator overnight. Heat through in a covered saucepan, stirring gently and adding a little water to ham if necessary.

COLORFUL MINESTRONE

This vegetarian soup features a rainbow of vegetables. In place of the spirals, use any multi-colored pasta.
—Crystal Schlueter Babbitt, MN

Prep: 20 min. • **Cook:** 6 hours 20 minutes
Makes: 10 servings (3¾ quarts)

4 stalks Swiss chard (about ½ pound)
2 tablespoons olive oil
1 medium red onion, finely chopped
6 cups vegetable broth
2 cans (14½ ounces each) fire-roasted diced tomatoes, undrained
1 can (16 ounces) kidney beans, rinsed and drained
1 can (15 ounces) chickpeas, rinsed and drained
1 medium yellow summer squash or zucchini, halved and cut into ¼-inch slices
1 medium sweet red or yellow pepper, finely chopped
1 medium carrot, finely chopped
2 garlic cloves, minced
1½ cups uncooked spiral pasta
¼ cup prepared pesto

1. Cut stems from chard; chop stems and leaves separately. Reserve leaves for adding later. In a large skillet, heat oil over medium heat. Add onion and the chard stems; cook and stir 3-5 minutes or until tender. Transfer to a 6-qt. slow cooker.
2. Stir in broth, tomatoes, beans, chickpeas, squash, pepper, carrot and garlic. Cook, covered, on low 6-8 hours or until vegetables are tender.
3. Stir in pasta and reserved chard leaves. Cook, covered, on low 20-25 minutes longer or until pasta is tender. Serve with pesto.

COLORFUL MINESTRONE

BRISKET SLIDERS WITH CARAMELIZED ONIONS

For a dear friend's going-away party, I made a juicy brisket and turned it into a few dozen sliders. Cook the brisket ahead of time and slider assembly will be a snap.
—**Marlies Coventry** North Vancouver, BC

Prep: 25 min. + marinating • **Cook:** 7 hours
Makes: 2 dozen

- **2 tablespoons plus ⅛ teaspoon salt, divided**
- **2 tablespoons sugar**
- **2 tablespoons whole peppercorns, crushed**
- **5 garlic cloves, minced**
- **1 fresh beef brisket (about 4 pounds)**
- **1 cup mayonnaise**
- **½ cup crumbled blue cheese**
- **2 teaspoons horseradish**
- **⅛ teaspoon cayenne pepper**
- **3 medium carrots, cut into 1-inch pieces**
- **2 medium onions, chopped**
- **2 celery ribs, chopped**
- **1 cup dry red wine or beef broth**
- **¼ cup stone-ground mustard**
- **3 bay leaves**
- **1 tablespoon olive oil**
- **3 medium onions, sliced**
- **24 mini buns**
- **Arugula and tomato slices, optional**

1. In a bowl, combine 2 tablespoons salt, sugar, peppercorns and garlic; rub onto all sides of brisket. Wrap brisket in plastic; refrigerate 8 hours or overnight. In a small bowl, combine the mayonnaise, blue cheese, horseradish and cayenne. Refrigerate until assembling.
2. Place carrots, chopped onions and celery in a 6- or 7-qt. slow cooker. Unwrap brisket; place on top of the vegetables. In a small bowl, combine red wine, mustard and bay leaves; pour over brisket. Cook, covered, on low 7-9 hours or until meat is fork-tender. Meanwhile, in a large skillet, heat oil over medium heat. Add sliced onions and remaining salt; cook and stir until softened. Reduce heat to medium-low; cook 30-35 minutes or until deep golden brown, stirring the mixture occasionally.
3. Remove brisket; cool slightly. Reserve 1 cup cooking juices; discard remaining juices. Skim fat from reserved juices. Thinly slice brisket across the grain; return to the slow cooker. Pour juices over brisket.
4. Serve the brisket on buns with mayonnaise mixture and caramelized onions and, if desired, arugula and tomato slices.

HEARTY MINESTRONE

I picked up this recipe in California in the '80s and have been making it ever since. I enjoy it partly because it's simple to put together and partly because the flavor is so wonderful!

—**Bonnie Hosman** Young, AZ

Prep: 25 min. • **Cook:** 6¼ hours
Makes: 7 servings (about 2½ quarts)

- **2 cans (one 28 ounces, one 14½ ounces) diced tomatoes, undrained**
- **2 cups water**
- **2 medium carrots, sliced**
- **1 medium onion, chopped**
- **1 medium zucchini, chopped**
- **1 package (3½ ounces) sliced pepperoni**
- **2 teaspoons minced garlic**
- **2 teaspoons chicken bouillon granules**
- **½ teaspoon dried basil**
- **½ teaspoon dried oregano**
- **2 cans (16 ounces each) kidney beans, rinsed and drained**
- **1 package (10 ounces) frozen chopped spinach, thawed and squeezed dry**
- **1¼ cups cooked elbow macaroni**
- **Shredded Parmesan cheese**

1. In a 5-qt. slow cooker, combine the first 10 ingredients. Cover and cook on low for 6-8 hours or until vegetables are tender.
2. Stir in the beans, spinach and macaroni. Cover and cook 15 minutes longer or until heated through. Sprinkle with cheese.

Freeze option: Cool soup and transfer to freezer containers. Freeze soup for up to 3 months. To use frozen soup, thaw in the refrigerator overnight. Transfer to a saucepan. Cover and cook over medium heat until heated through. Sprinkle with the cheese.

BBQ CHICKEN SLIDERS

Brining the chicken overnight helps it taste exceptionally good, making it so tender it practically melts in your mouth.

—**Rachel Kunkel** Schell City, MO

Prep: 25 min. + brining • **Cook:** 4 hours
Makes: 8 servings (2 sliders each)

BRINE

- **1½ quarts water**
- **¼ cup packed brown sugar**
- **2 tablespoons salt**
- **1 tablespoon liquid smoke**
- **2 garlic cloves, minced**
- **½ teaspoon dried thyme**

CHICKEN

- **2 pounds boneless skinless chicken breasts**
- **⅓ cup liquid smoke**
- **1½ cups hickory smoke-flavored barbecue sauce**
- **16 slider buns or dinner rolls, split and warmed**

1. In a large bowl, mix brine ingredients, stirring to dissolve brown sugar. Reserve 1 cup brine for cooking chicken; cover and refrigerate.
2. Place chicken in a large resealable bag; add remaining brine. Seal bag, pressing out as much air as possible; turn to coat chicken. Place in a large bowl; refrigerate 18-24 hours, turning occasionally.
3. Remove chicken from brine and transfer to a 3-qt. slow cooker; discard brine in bag. Add reserved 1 cup brine and ⅓ cup liquid smoke to chicken. Cook, covered, on low for 4-5 hours or until chicken is tender.
4. Remove chicken; cool slightly. Discard cooking juices. Shred chicken with two forks and return to slow cooker. Stir in barbecue sauce; heat through. Serve chicken on buns.

BBQ CHICKEN SLIDERS

MARYLAND-STYLE CRAB SOUP

MARYLAND-STYLE CRAB SOUP

Try this hearty change-of-pace soup that incorporates flavorful crab into the best vegetable soup ever. I break whole crabs and claws into pieces and drop them into the soup to cook for even more flavor. Saltine crackers and ice-cold beer are all you need to serve alongside.
—**Freelove Knott** Palm Bay, FL

Prep: 20 min. • **Cook:** 6¼ hours
Makes: 8 servings (3 quarts)

- **2 cans (14½ ounces each) diced tomatoes with green peppers and onions, undrained**
- **2 cups water**
- **1½ pounds potatoes, cut into ½-inch cubes (about 5 cups)**
- **2 cups cubed peeled rutabaga**
- **2 cups chopped cabbage**
- **1 medium onion, finely chopped**
- **1 medium carrot, sliced**
- **½ cup frozen corn, thawed**
- **½ cup frozen lima beans, thawed**
- **½ cup frozen peas, thawed**
- **½ cup cut fresh green beans (1-inch pieces)**
- **4 teaspoons seafood seasoning**
- **1 teaspoon celery seed**
- **1 vegetable bouillon cube**
- **¼ teaspoon salt**
- **¼ teaspoon pepper**
- **1 pound fresh or lump crabmeat, drained**

1. In a 6-qt. slow cooker, combine the first 16 ingredients. Cook, covered, on low 6-8 hours or until the vegetables are tender.
2. Stir in crab. Cook, covered, on low 15 minutes longer or until heated through.

Note: This recipe was prepared with Knorr vegetable bouillon.

SLOW-COOKED BARBECUED PORK SANDWICHES

These saucy sandwiches are great for a hungry crowd and easy to prepare. Just keep the meat warm in the slow cooker until it's time to serve.
—**Kimberly Wallace** Dennison, OH

Prep: 20 min. • **Cook:** 7 hours
Makes: 10 servings

- **1 medium onion, chopped**
- **1 tablespoon butter**
- **1 can (15 ounces) tomato puree**
- **½ cup packed brown sugar**
- **¼ cup steak sauce**
- **2 tablespoons lemon juice**
- **½ teaspoon salt**
- **1 boneless pork shoulder butt roast (3 pounds)**
- **10 hard rolls, split**
- **Coleslaw, optional**

1. In a large skillet, saute onion in butter until tender. Stir in the tomato puree, brown sugar, steak sauce, lemon juice and salt. Cook over medium heat until sugar is dissolved and heated through.
2. Place roast in a 5-qt. slow cooker; pour sauce over the top. Cover and cook on low for 7-9 hours or until meat is tender. Remove roast; cool slightly. Skim fat from cooking juices. Shred meat with two forks and return to the slow cooker; heat through. Serve on rolls. Top with coleslaw if desired.

★★★★★ **READER REVIEW**

"I made this today and it was great! My 4-year-old had two servings. I just couldn't believe how good this was with such little seasoning. I set onions, pickles and peppers on the side to put on the sandwiches."

MEAGANTEAL TASTEOFHOME.COM

HOT PINEAPPLE HAM SANDWICHES

PORK & RICE NOODLE SOUP

My husband and I are crazy over the Korean noodle bowls at our favorite restaurant. I created this recipe to enjoy the same flavors in a quick and easy meal. You can find rice noodles in the Asian section of the grocery store.
—**Lisa Renshaw** Kansas City, MO

Prep: 15 min. • **Cook:** 6½ hours
Makes: 8 servings (3 quarts)

- **1½ pounds boneless country-style pork ribs, cut into 1-inch cubes**
- **6 garlic cloves, minced**
- **2 tablespoons minced fresh gingerroot**
- **2 cans (14½ ounces each) reduced-sodium chicken broth**
- **2 cans (13.66 ounces each) coconut milk**
- **¼ cup reduced-sodium soy sauce**
- **4 ounces uncooked thin rice noodles**
- **2 cups frozen pepper strips, thawed**
- **1 can (8 ounces) sliced water chestnuts, drained**
- **¼ cup minced fresh cilantro**
- **2 tablespoons lime juice**

1. In a 5-qt. slow cooker, combine the first six ingredients. Cook, covered, on low 6-8 hours or until meat is tender.
2. Add rice noodles, pepper strips and water chestnuts; cook 30-35 minutes longer or until noodles are tender. If desired, skim soup. Just before serving, stir in cilantro and lime juice.

*

TEST KITCHEN TIP

Be sure you're using the correct slow cooker for the job! Always read the recipe's directions first to be sure your slow cooker is the proper size. Slow cookers should be half to two-thirds full to ensure proper cooking of food.

HOT PINEAPPLE HAM SANDWICHES

Your trusty slow cooker lets you make these warm, gooey sandwiches without heating up the house on a warm day. The mustard and brown sugar give them a satisfying richness.
—**Nancy Foust** Stoneboro, PA

Prep: 25 min. • **Cook:** 3 hours
Makes: 10 servings

- **2 cans (20 ounces each) unsweetened crushed pineapple, undrained**
- **1 medium onion, finely chopped**
- **¾ cup packed light brown sugar**
- **¼ cup Dijon mustard**
- **2½ pounds thinly sliced deli ham**
- **2 tablespoons cornstarch**
- **2 tablespoons water**
- **10 slices Swiss cheese or cheddar cheese, optional**
- **10 kaiser rolls, split**

1. In a large bowl, combine the first four ingredients. Place half of the mixture in a 5-qt. slow cooker; top with half of the ham. Repeat layers. Cook, covered, on low until heated through, 3-4 hours.
2. Using tongs, remove ham from slow cooker to a platter. Cover ham with foil. Keep the pineapple mixture in the slow cooker.
3. In a large saucepan, combine the cornstarch and water until smooth. Stir in pineapple mixture; bring to a boil. Reduce heat; simmer, uncovered, until mixture is slightly thickened, stirring occasionally.
4. Serve ham, pineapple mixture and, if desired, cheese on rolls.

PORK & RICE NOODLE SOUP

ASIAN SHREDDED PORK SANDWICHES

On cool-weather weeknights, the slow cooker is our friend. The plums might surprise in these juicy pork sandwiches, but they add a little sweetness and make the meat extra tender.

—**Holly Battiste** Barrington, NJ

Prep: 30 min. • **Cook:** 6 hours
Makes: 10 servings

- **1 can (15 ounces) plums, drained and pitted**
- **1 tablespoon Sriracha Asian hot chili sauce**
- **1 tablespoon hoisin sauce**
- **1 tablespoon reduced-sodium soy sauce**
- **1 tablespoon rice vinegar**
- **1 tablespoon honey**
- **2 garlic cloves, minced**
- **1 teaspoon pepper**
- **1 teaspoon sesame oil**
- **½ teaspoon ground ginger**
- **¼ teaspoon salt**
- **2 tablespoons canola oil**
- **1 boneless pork shoulder butt roast (3 pounds)**
- **4 medium carrots, finely chopped**
- **10 ciabatta rolls, split**
- **Shredded napa or other cabbage**

1. In a large bowl, mix the first 11 ingredients. In a large skillet, heat the oil over medium-high heat. Brown roast on all sides.
2. Place carrots in a 4- or 5-qt. slow cooker. Add roast; pour plum mixture over top. Cook, covered, on low until pork is tender, 6-8 hours.
3. Remove pork; shred with two forks. Skim fat from carrot mixture; stir in pork and heat through. Serve mixture on rolls with cabbage.

Freeze option: Freeze cooled pork mixture in freezer containers. To use, partially thaw in refrigerator overnight. Heat through in a covered saucepan, stirring gently and adding a little broth if necessary.

*

TEST KITCHEN TIP

For individual sandwiches at the ready, set the cooked pork mixture in the refrigerator overnight. The following day, mound the pork in ½ - to 1-cup servings on a baking sheet. Cover and freeze. When frozen, pop the mounds off the sheet and store in a resealable freezer storage bag. Then it's a cinch to reheat a serving in the microwave when you need a fast sandwich.

GYRO SOUP

If you're a fan of lamb, don't pass up this Greek-style soup. Seasoned with the classic flavors of rosemary, marjoram and mint, it transports you straight to the glorious Mediterranean.

—**Bridget Klusman** Otsego, MI

Prep: 25 min. • **Cook:** 6 hours
Makes: 6 servings

- **2 pounds ground lamb**
- **5 cups water**
- **1 can (14½ ounces) diced tomatoes, undrained**
- **1 medium onion, chopped**
- **¼ cup red wine**
- **6 garlic cloves, minced**
- **3 tablespoons minced fresh mint or 1 tablespoon dried mint**
- **1 tablespoon dried marjoram**
- **1 tablespoon dried rosemary, crushed**
- **2 teaspoons salt**
- **½ teaspoon pepper**
- **Optional toppings: plain Greek yogurt and crumbled feta cheese**

1. In a large skillet, cook and crumble lamb over medium-high heat until no longer pink, 8-10 minutes. Using a slotted spoon, transfer lamb to a 4- or 5-qt. slow cooker. Stir in water, tomatoes, onion, wine, garlic, herbs, salt and pepper.
2. Cook, covered, on low until flavors are blended, 6-8 hours. Serve with toppings as desired.

Freeze option: Freeze cooled soup in freezer containers. To use, partially thaw in refrigerator overnight. Heat through in a saucepan, stirring occasionally.

GYRO SOUP

TROPICAL PULLED PORK SLIDERS

I used what I had in my cupboard to make this Hawaiian-style pork filling, and the results were fantastic. It's a delicious way to fuel up at a party.

—**Shelly Mitchell** Gresham, OR

Prep: 15 min. • **Cook:** 8 hours
Makes: 12 servings

- **1 boneless pork shoulder butt roast (3 pounds)**
- **2 garlic cloves, minced**
- **½ teaspoon lemon-pepper seasoning**
- **1 can (20 ounces) unsweetened crushed pineapple, undrained**
- **½ cup orange juice**
- **1 jar (16 ounces) mango salsa**
- **24 whole wheat dinner rolls, split**

1. Rub roast with garlic and lemon pepper. Transfer to a 4-qt. slow cooker; top with pineapple and orange juice. Cook, covered, on low 8-10 hours or until meat is tender.
2. Remove roast; cool slightly. Skim fat from cooking juices. Shred pork with two forks. Return pork and cooking juices to slow cooker. Stir in salsa; heat through. Serve with rolls.

SLOW COOKER
BEEF TOSTADAS

MAIN DISHES

Looking for comfort or convenience (or a little of both)? These savory dishes answer all of your dinnertime dilemmas. Dig in to these new family favorites tonight!

SLOW COOKER BEEF TOSTADAS

I dedicate these yummy slow-simmered tostadas to my husband, the only Italian man I know who can't get enough of Mexican flavors. Pile on your favorite toppings and enjoy!

—**Teresa DeVono** Red Lion, PA

Prep: 20 min. • **Cook:** 6 hours
Makes: 6 servings

- 1 large onion, chopped
- ¼ cup lime juice
- 1 jalapeno pepper, seeded and minced
- 1 serrano pepper, seeded and minced
- 1 tablespoon chili powder
- 3 garlic cloves, minced
- ½ teaspoon ground cumin
- 1 beef top round steak (about 1½ pounds)
- 1 teaspoon salt
- ½ teaspoon pepper
- ¼ cup chopped fresh cilantro
- 12 corn tortillas (6 inches)
- Cooking spray

TOPPINGS

- 1½ cups shredded lettuce
- 1 medium tomato, finely chopped
- ¾ cup shredded sharp cheddar cheese
- ¾ cup reduced-fat sour cream, optional

1. Place the first seven ingredients in a 3- or 4-qt. slow cooker. Cut steak in half and sprinkle with salt and pepper; add to slow cooker. Cook, covered, on low until meat is tender, 6-8 hours.
2. Remove meat; cool slightly. Shred meat with two forks. Return beef to slow cooker and stir in cilantro; heat through. Spritz both sides of tortillas with cooking spray. Place in a single layer on baking sheets; broil for 1-2 minutes on each side or until crisp. Spoon beef mixture over tortillas; top with lettuce, tomato, cheese and, if desired, sour cream.

Note: Wear disposable gloves when cutting hot peppers; the oils can burn skin. Avoid touching your face.

THAI SHRIMP & RICE

Raisins and coconut milk add a lovely hint of sweetness to shrimp, while fresh lime and ginger give it a wonderful aroma. It adds a fun flair to weeknight menus.

—**Paula Marchesi** Lenhartsville, PA

Prep: 30 min. • **Cook:** 3¼ hours
Makes: 8 servings

- 2 cans (14½ ounces each) chicken broth
- 2 cups uncooked converted rice
- 1 large carrot, shredded
- 1 medium onion, chopped
- ½ cup each chopped green and sweet red pepper
- ½ cup water
- ½ cup coconut milk
- ⅓ cup lime juice
- ¼ cup sweetened shredded coconut
- ¼ cup each raisins and golden raisins
- 8 garlic cloves, minced
- 1 tablespoon grated lime peel
- 1 tablespoon minced fresh gingerroot
- 1 teaspoon salt
- 1 teaspoon each ground coriander and cumin
- ½ teaspoon cayenne pepper
- 1 pound cooked medium shrimp, peeled and deveined
- ½ cup fresh snow peas, cut into thin strips

1. In a 5-qt. slow cooker, combine the broth, rice, vegetables, water, coconut milk, lime juice, coconut, raisins, garlic, lime peel and seasonings. Cover and cook on low for 3 hours or until rice is tender.
2. Stir in shrimp and peas. Cover and cook 15-20 minutes longer or until heated through.

*

TEST KITCHEN TIP

Converted white rice, also called parboiled rice, is grain that has been steam-pressured before it is milled to remove the hull. This process retains nutrients and makes fluffy separated grains of cooked rice. Converted rice takes a bit longer to cook than regular long grain rice, making it an ideal addition to slow-cooked recipes.

CARIBBEAN CHICKEN STEW

I lived with a West Indian family for awhile and enjoyed their food so much. Here's a favorite I lightened up by leaving out the oil and sugar, removing the chicken skin and using chicken sausage.
—Joanne Iovino Kings Park, NY

Prep: 25 min. + marinating • **Cook:** 6 hours
Makes: 8 servings

- **¼ cup ketchup**
- **3 garlic cloves, minced**
- **1 tablespoon sugar**
- **1 tablespoon hot pepper sauce**
- **1 teaspoon browning sauce, optional**
- **1 teaspoon dried basil**
- **1 teaspoon dried thyme**
- **1 teaspoon paprika**
- **½ teaspoon salt**
- **½ teaspoon dried oregano**
- **½ teaspoon ground allspice**
- **½ teaspoon pepper**
- **8 bone-in chicken thighs (about 3 pounds), skin removed**
- **1 pound fully cooked andouille chicken sausage links, sliced**
- **1 medium onion, finely chopped**
- **2 medium carrots, finely chopped**
- **2 celery ribs, finely chopped**

1. In a large resealable plastic bag, combine ketchup, garlic, sugar, pepper sauce and, if desired, browning sauce; stir in seasonings. Add the chicken thighs, sausage and vegetables. Seal bag and turn to coat. Refrigerate 8 hours or overnight.
2. Transfer contents of bag to a 4- or 5-qt. slow cooker. Cook, covered, on low 6-8 hours or until chicken is tender.

BEEF BRISKET IN BEER

One bite of this super tender brisket, and your family will be hooked! The rich gravy is perfect for spooning over some creamy mashed potatoes, noodles or rice.

—**Eunice Stoen** Decorah, IA

Prep: 15 min. • **Cook:** 8 hours
Makes: 6 servings

- **1 fresh beef brisket (2½ to 3 pounds)**
- **2 teaspoons liquid smoke, optional**
- **1 teaspoon celery salt**
- **½ teaspoon pepper**
- **¼ teaspoon salt**
- **1 large onion, sliced**
- **1 can (12 ounces) beer or nonalcoholic beer**
- **2 teaspoons Worcestershire sauce**
- **2 tablespoons cornstarch**
- **¼ cup cold water**

1. Cut brisket in half; rub with liquid smoke, if desired, and celery salt, pepper and salt. Place in a 3-qt. slow cooker. Top with onion. Combine beer and Worcestershire sauce; pour over meat. Cover and cook on low for 8-9 hours or until tender.

2. Remove the brisket and keep warm. Strain cooking juices; transfer to a small saucepan. In a small bowl, combine cornstarch and water until smooth; stir into juices. Bring to a boil; cook and stir for 2 minutes or until thickened. Serve beef with gravy.

Note: This is a fresh beef brisket, not corned beef.

*

TEST KITCHEN TIP

Liquid smoke is a great addition to this recipe as it adds depth of flavor. Be careful not to overdo it; a small amount goes a long way. Look for liquid smoke in your grocery store near the spices and marinades.

BEEF BRISKET IN BEER

PINEAPPLE CURRY CHICKEN

Curry has a moderate to strong delivery, so add it early in the cooking process for good balance with the pineapple, coconut and ginger.

—**Robin Haas** Cranston, RI

Prep: 25 min. • **Cook:** 6 hours
Makes: 6 servings

- **2 cans (8 ounces each) unsweetened pineapple chunks, undrained**
- **6 bone-in chicken breast halves, skin removed (12 ounces each)**
- **1 can (15 ounces) garbanzo beans, rinsed and drained**
- **1 large onion, cut into 1-inch pieces**
- **1 cup julienned carrots**
- **1 medium sweet red pepper, cut into strips**
- **½ cup light coconut milk**
- **2 tablespoons cornstarch**
- **2 tablespoons sugar**
- **3 teaspoons curry powder**
- **2 garlic cloves, minced**
- **2 teaspoons minced fresh gingerroot**
- **1 teaspoon salt**
- **1 teaspoon pepper**
- **1 teaspoon lime juice**
- **½ teaspoon crushed red pepper flakes**
- **Hot cooked rice**
- **⅓ cup minced fresh basil**
- **Toasted sweetened shredded coconut, optional**

1. Drain pineapple, reserving ¾ cup juice. Place the chicken, beans, vegetables and pineapple in a 6-qt. slow cooker. In a small bowl, combine the coconut milk and cornstarch until smooth.

2. Stir in the sugar, curry powder, garlic, ginger, salt, pepper, lime juice, pepper flakes and reserved juice; pour mixture over the chicken.

3. Cover and cook on low for 6-8 hours or until chicken is tender. Serve with cooked rice; sprinkle with basil and, if desired, coconut.

ZIPPY SPAGHETTI SAUCE

This thick and hearty sauce goes a long way to fill my hungry family. They enjoy any leftovers ladled over thick slices of grilled garlic bread. To make sure I have the ingredients on hand, I keep a bag of chopped green pepper in my freezer and minced garlic in my fridge—always!
—Elaine Priest Dover, PA

Prep: 20 min. • **Cook:** 6 hours
Makes: about 3 quarts

- **2 pounds ground beef**
- **1 cup chopped onion**
- **½ cup chopped green pepper**
- **2 cans (15 ounces each) tomato sauce**
- **1 can (28 ounces) diced tomatoes, undrained**
- **1 can (12 ounces) tomato paste**
- **½ pound sliced fresh mushrooms**
- **1 cup grated Parmesan cheese**
- **½ to ¾ cup dry red wine or beef broth**
- **½ cup sliced pimiento-stuffed olives**
- **¼ cup dried parsley flakes**
- **1 to 2 tablespoons dried oregano**
- **2 teaspoons Italian seasoning**
- **2 teaspoons minced garlic**
- **1 teaspoon salt**
- **1 teaspoon pepper**
- **Hot cooked spaghetti**

1. In a large skillet, cook the beef, onion and green pepper over medium heat until meat is no longer pink; drain.
2. Transfer to a 5-qt. slow cooker. Stir in the tomato sauce, tomatoes, tomato paste, mushrooms, cheese, wine, olives, parsley, oregano, Italian seasoning, garlic, salt and pepper. Cover and cook on low for 6-8 hours. Serve with spaghetti.

DID YOU KNOW?

You can make your own Italian seasoning blend. A basic blend might contain marjoram, thyme, rosemary, savory, sage, oregano and basil. To get started try substituting ¼ teaspoon each of basil, thyme, rosemary and oregano for each teaspoon of Italian seasoning called for in a recipe.

BUSY-DAY CHICKEN FAJITAS

When I don't have much time to cook supper, chicken fajitas from the slow cooker are a flavorful way to keep my family satisfied. If you aren't cooking for youngsters, try spicing things up with medium or hot picante sauce.
—Michele Furry Plains, MT

Prep: 20 min. • **Cook:** 4 hours
Makes: 6 servings

- **1 pound boneless skinless chicken breasts**
- **1 can (15 ounces) black beans, rinsed and drained**
- **1 medium green pepper, cut into strips**
- **1 large onion, sliced**
- **1½ cups picante sauce**
- **½ teaspoon garlic powder**
- **½ teaspoon ground cumin**
- **12 flour tortillas (6 inches), warmed**
- **2 cups shredded cheddar cheese**
- **Optional toppings: thinly sliced green onions, chopped tomatoes and sour cream, optional**

1. Place chicken in a 4-qt. slow cooker; add black beans, pepper and onion. In a small bowl, mix picante sauce, garlic powder and cumin; pour over top. Cook, covered, on low 4-5 hours or until chicken is tender.
2. Carefully remove chicken and cool slightly. Shred meat with two forks and return to slow cooker; heat through. Serve with tortillas, cheese and toppings of your choice.

ZIPPY SPAGHETTI SAUCE

SAUSAGE WITH JALAPENO POTATOES

SAUSAGE WITH JALAPENO POTATOES

Wow! This flavor-packed recipe really stands out from typical sausage dishes. Cut back on the jalapenos if you'd like.
—**Rose Smith** Royalton, IL

Prep: 25 min. • **Cook:** 5 hours
Makes: 6 servings

- 3 **pounds potatoes (about 6 medium), peeled and cut into 1-inch cubes**
- 3 **jalapeno peppers, sliced and seeded**
- ¼ **cup butter, cubed**
- 2 **tablespoons water**
- 3 **garlic cloves, minced**
- ¾ **teaspoon salt**
- ¼ **teaspoon pepper**
- 2 **medium sweet red peppers, halved and cut into 1-inch strips**
- 2 **medium sweet yellow or orange peppers, halved and cut into 1-inch strips**
- 1 **large onion, halved and thinly sliced**
- 1 **teaspoon olive oil**
- 5 **Italian sausage links (4 ounces each)**
- **Chopped fresh basil, optional**

1. Place the first seven ingredients in a 6-qt. slow cooker; toss to combine. Top with sweet peppers and onion.
2. In a skillet, heat oil over medium-high heat. Brown sausages on all sides; place over vegetables. Cook, covered, on low 5-6 hours or until potatoes are tender.
3. Remove sausages; cut diagonally into 2- to 3-in. pieces. Remove vegetables with a slotted spoon; serve with sausage. If desired, sprinkle with basil.

Note: Wear disposable gloves when cutting hot peppers; the oils can burn skin. Avoid touching your face.

*

TEST KITCHEN TIP

This meal-in-one dish is perfect for busy family cooks because the starch, protein and veggies simmer together. If you're looking to round out the meal, however, consider serving wedges of warm cornbread.

SLOW COOKER TROPICAL PORK CHOPS

Savory pork and sweet fruits go so nicely together. Cook them slowly, then add fresh herbs right before serving for a light, bright main dish.
—**Roxanne Chan** Albany, CA

Prep: 15 min. • **Cook:** 3 hours
Makes: 4 servings

- **2 jars (23½ ounces each) mixed tropical fruit, drained and chopped**
- **¾ cup thawed limeade concentrate**
- **¼ cup sweet chili sauce**
- **1 garlic clove, minced**
- **1 teaspoon minced fresh gingerroot**
- **4 bone-in pork loin chops (¾ inch thick and 5 ounces each)**
- **1 green onion, finely chopped**
- **2 tablespoons minced fresh cilantro**
- **2 tablespoons minced fresh mint**
- **2 tablespoons slivered almonds, toasted**
- **2 tablespoons finely chopped crystallized ginger, optional**
- **½ teaspoon grated lime peel**

1. In a 3-qt. slow cooker, combine the first five ingredients. Add pork, arranging chops to sit snugly in fruit mixture. Cook, covered, on low 3-4 hours or until meat is tender (a thermometer inserted in pork should read at least 145°).
2. In a small bowl, mix the remaining ingredients. To serve, remove pork chops from slow cooker. Using a slotted spoon, serve fruit over pork. Sprinkle with the herb mixture.

Note: To toast nuts, place them in a dry nonstick skillet and heat over low heat until lightly browned, stirring occasionally.

SLOW COOKER TROPICAL PORK CHOPS

STEAK SAN MARINO

I'm a busy pastor's wife and mother of three, and this delicious, inexpensive dish helps my day run smoother. The steak is so tender and flavorful, my kids gobble it up and my husband asks for seconds.
—**Lael Griess** Hull, IA

Prep: 15 min. • **Cook:** 7 hours
Makes: 6 servings

- **¼ cup all-purpose flour**
- **½ teaspoon salt**
- **½ teaspoon pepper**
- **1 beef top round steak (1½ pounds), cut into six pieces**
- **2 large carrots, sliced**
- **1 celery rib, sliced**
- **1 can (8 ounces) tomato sauce**
- **2 garlic cloves, minced**
- **1 bay leaf**
- **1 teaspoon Italian seasoning**
- **½ teaspoon Worcestershire sauce**
- **3 cups hot cooked brown rice**

1. In a large resealable plastic bag, combine the flour, salt and pepper. Add beef, a few pieces at a time, and shake to coat. Transfer to a 4-qt. slow cooker.
2. In a small bowl, combine the carrots, celery, tomato sauce, garlic, bay leaf, Italian seasoning and Worcestershire sauce. Pour over beef. Cover and cook on low for 7-9 hours or until beef is tender. Discard bay leaf. Serve with rice.

Freeze option: Place cooked steak and vegetables in freezer containers; top with sauce. Cool and freeze. To use, partially thaw in refrigerator overnight. Heat through in a covered saucepan, gently stirring and adding a little water to the mixture if necessary.

CONGA LIME PORK

Dinner guests won't be shy to get in the buffet line when this dish makes an appearance. The pork roast is dressed in sauce that has chipotle and molasses, making it a tasty change of pace.
—**Janice Elder** Charlotte, NC

Prep: 20 min. • **Cook:** 4 hours
Makes: 6 servings

- **1 teaspoon salt, divided**
- **½ teaspoon pepper, divided**
- **1 boneless pork shoulder butt roast (2 to 3 pounds)**
- **1 tablespoon canola oil**
- **1 large onion, chopped**
- **3 garlic cloves, peeled and thinly sliced**
- **½ cup water**
- **2 chipotle peppers in adobo sauce, seeded and chopped**
- **2 tablespoons molasses**
- **2 cups broccoli coleslaw mix**
- **1 medium mango, peeled and chopped**
- **2 tablespoons lime juice**
- **1½ teaspoons grated lime peel**
- **6 prepared corn muffins, halved**
- **Lime wedges, optional**

1. Sprinkle ¾ teaspoon salt and ¼ teaspoon pepper over the roast. In a large skillet, brown pork in oil on all sides. Transfer the meat to a 3- or 4-qt. slow cooker.
2. In the same skillet, saute onion until tender. Add garlic; cook 1 minute longer. Add the water, chipotle peppers and molasses, stirring to loosen browned bits from pan. Pour over pork. Cover and cook on high for 4-5 hours or until meat is tender.
3. Remove roast; cool slightly. Skim fat from cooking juices. Shred pork with two forks and return to slow cooker; heat through. In a large bowl, combine the coleslaw mix, mango, lime juice, lime peel and remaining salt and pepper.
4. Place muffin halves cut side down on an ungreased baking sheet. Broil 4 in. from the heat for 2-3 minutes or until lightly toasted. Serve pork with muffins and, if desired, lime wedges; top with the slaw.

PEPPERY CHICKEN WITH POTATOES

We like this recipe on Sundays because the chicken simmers on its own and is ready when we get home from church.
—**Lori Draves** Highland, WI

Prep: 20 min. • **Cook:** 5 hours + standing
Makes: 4 servings

- **1 pound red potatoes (about 6 medium), cut into wedges**
- **1 large onion, chopped**
- **2 teaspoons salt**
- **1 teaspoon paprika**
- **½ teaspoon onion powder**
- **½ teaspoon garlic powder**
- **½ teaspoon dried thyme**
- **½ teaspoon white pepper**
- **½ teaspoon cayenne pepper**
- **¼ teaspoon pepper**
- **1 broiler/fryer chicken (3½ to 4 pounds)**

1. Place potatoes and onion in a 6-qt. slow cooker. In a small bowl, mix the seasonings. Tuck wings under chicken; tie drumsticks together. Rub seasoning mixture over outside and inside of chicken. Place chicken over vegetables.
2. Cook, covered, on low 5-6 hours or until a thermometer inserted in thickest part of thigh reads 170°-175°. Remove chicken from slow cooker; tent with foil. Let stand 15 minutes before carving.
3. Transfer vegetables to a platter; keep warm. If desired, skim fat and thicken cooking juices for gravy. Serve with the chicken.

PEPPERY CHICKEN WITH POTATOES

ITALIAN SHRIMP & PASTA

This dish will remind you a bit of classic shrimp creole, but it has a surprise Italian twist. Slow cooking gives it hands-off ease. It's perfect for a small dinner party.
—Karen Edwards Sanford, ME

Prep: 20 min. • **Cook:** 7½ hours
Makes: 6 servings

- **1 pound boneless skinless chicken thighs, cut into 2x1-in. strips**
- **2 tablespoons canola oil**
- **1 can (28 ounces) crushed tomatoes**
- **2 celery ribs, chopped**
- **1 medium green pepper, cut into 1-inch pieces**
- **1 medium onion, coarsely chopped**
- **2 garlic cloves, minced**
- **1 tablespoon sugar**
- **½ teaspoon salt**
- **½ teaspoon Italian seasoning**
- **⅛ to ¼ teaspoon cayenne pepper**
- **1 bay leaf**
- **1 cup uncooked orzo or other small pasta**
- **1 pound cooked medium shrimp, peeled and deveined**

1. In a large skillet, brown chicken in oil; transfer to a 3-qt. slow cooker. Stir in tomatoes, celery, pepper, onion, garlic, sugar and seasonings. Cook, covered, on low for 7-8 hours or until the chicken is just tender.
2. Discard bay leaf. Stir in pasta; cook, covered, on high for 15 minutes or until pasta is tender. Stir in the shrimp; cook, covered, 5 minutes longer or until the mixture is heated through.

*

TEST KITCHEN TIP

Orzo is a firm, mild-flavored rice-shaped pasta. It holds up well to long simmering times, making it ideal in slow cooker recipes. Look for orzo in the pasta aisle of the grocery store.

LIME CHICKEN TACOS

Our fun, simple recipe is perfect for taco Tuesdays or a relaxing dinner with friends. If we have any leftover filling, I toss it into a garden-fresh taco salad.
—Tracy Gunter Boise, ID

Prep: 10 min. • **Cook:** 5½ hours
Makes: 6 servings

- **1½ pounds boneless skinless chicken breast halves**
- **3 tablespoons lime juice**
- **1 tablespoon chili powder**
- **1 cup frozen corn, thawed**
- **1 cup chunky salsa**
- **12 fat-free flour tortillas (6 inches), warmed**
- **Sour cream, pickled onions, shredded lettuce, and shredded cheddar or cotija cheese, optional**

1. Place chicken in a 3-qt. slow cooker. Combine the lime juice and chili powder; pour over chicken. Cook, covered, on low until chicken is tender, 5-6 hours.
2. Remove chicken. When cool enough to handle, shred meat with two forks; return to slow cooker. Stir in corn and salsa. Cook, covered, on low until heated through, about 30 minutes. Place filling on tortillas; if desired, serve the tacos with sour cream, pickled onions, lettuce and cheese.

BBQ CHICKEN

BBQ CHICKEN

Of all the recipes that I make in my slow cooker, this is my favorite. If you like your BBQ sweet with a little spice, this will be your new go-to.

—Yvonne McKim Vancouver, WA

Prep: 15 min. • **Cook:** 5 hours
Makes: 12 servings

- **6 chicken leg quarters, skin removed**
- **¾ cup ketchup**
- **½ cup orange juice**
- **¼ cup packed brown sugar**
- **¼ cup red wine vinegar**
- **¼ cup olive oil**
- **4 teaspoons minced fresh parsley**
- **2 teaspoons Worcestershire sauce**
- **1 teaspoon garlic salt**
- **½ teaspoon pepper**
- **2 tablespoons plus 2 teaspoons cornstarch**
- **¼ cup water**

1. Using a sharp knife, cut through the joint of each leg quarter to separate into two pieces. Place the chicken in a 4-qt. slow cooker.
2. In a small bowl, mix ketchup, orange juice, brown sugar, vinegar, oil, parsley, Worcestershire sauce, garlic salt and pepper; pour over the chicken. Cook, covered, on low for 5-6 hours or until meat is tender.
3. Remove chicken to a serving platter; keep warm. Skim fat from cooking juices; pour into a measuring cup to measure 2 cups. Transfer to a small saucepan; bring to a boil.
4. In a small bowl, mix the cornstarch and water until smooth; stir into the cooking juices. Return to a boil, stirring constantly; cook and stir 1-2 minutes or until thickened. Serve with chicken.

CHEESY TURKEY MEAT LOAF

CHEESY TURKEY MEAT LOAF

Nothing says comfort food better than meat loaf! Get this one started in the morning and you'll have a delicious hot meal ready for lunch.

—Deanna Martinez-Bey Wake Forest, NC

Prep: 15 min. • **Cook:** 3 hours + standing
Makes: 6 servings

- **1 large egg, lightly beaten**
- **1 cup crushed saltines**
- **1 cup ketchup**
- **2 garlic cloves, minced**
- **1 teaspoon salt**
- **1 teaspoon pepper**
- **2 pounds ground turkey**
- **2½ cups shredded cheddar cheese, divided**
- **½ cup shredded Parmesan cheese**

1. Fold an 18-in. square piece of heavy-duty foil in half to make an 18x9-in. strip. Place strip on bottom and up sides of a 5- or 6-qt. slow cooker. Coat strip with cooking spray.
2. In a large bowl, combine the first six ingredients. Add turkey, 2 cups cheddar cheese and Parmesan cheese; mix lightly but thoroughly (mixture will be moist). Shape meat into an 8x5-in. loaf; place in center of strip.
3. Cook, covered, on low 3-4 hours or until a thermometer reads 165°. Sprinkle with remaining cheese during the last 20 minutes of cooking. Using ends of foil strip as handles, remove meat loaf to a platter. Let stand 15 minutes.

Freeze option: Prepare meat loaf as directed, omitting cheddar cheese over top. Securely wrap cooled meat loaf in plastic wrap and foil, then freeze. Freeze cheese in a freezer container. To use, partially thaw in refrigerator overnight. Unwrap meat loaf; reheat on a greased 15x10x1-in. baking pan in a preheated 350° oven until heated through and a thermometer inserted in center reads 165°. Sprinkle with cheese.

POTATO PIZZA CASSEROLE

Here's a fun, full-flavored meal the whole family will go for. It's great on weeknights when everyone comes through the door hungry at the same time.

—Tyler Sherman Williamsburg, VA

Prep: 25 min. • **Cook:** 4 hours
Makes: 8 servings

- **1 pound ground beef**
- **½ pound sliced fresh mushrooms**
- **1 medium green pepper, chopped**
- **1 small onion, chopped**
- **2 jars (14 ounces each) pizza sauce**
- **1 can (10¾ ounces) condensed cheddar cheese soup, undiluted**
- **½ cup 2% milk**
- **1 teaspoon Italian seasoning**
- **½ teaspoon garlic salt**
- **¼ teaspoon crushed red pepper flakes**
- **1 package (32 ounces) frozen cubed hash brown potatoes, thawed**
- **15 slices pepperoni, chopped**
- **2 cups shredded Italian cheese blend**

1. In a large skillet, cook the beef, mushrooms, green pepper and onion until meat is no longer pink; drain.
2. Meanwhile, in a large bowl, combine the pizza sauce, soup, milk, Italian seasoning, garlic salt and pepper flakes. Stir in the potatoes, pepperoni and the beef mixture.
3. Transfer half of the mixture to a 5-qt slow cooker. Sprinkle with half of the cheese; repeat layers. Cover and cook on low for 4-5 hours or until the potatoes are tender.

★★★★★ **READER REVIEW**

"I wasn't sure how the potatoes would add to this dish but even my picker eater ate this one up. It was so easy to prepare, too!"

SBHKC90 TASTEOFHOME.COM

MEAT SAUCE FOR SPAGHETTI

MEAT SAUCE FOR SPAGHETTI

This hearty meat sauce turns ordinary spaghetti into a feast. If you do not have spaghetti noodles, no problem! I've successfully swirled up this sauce with nearly every pasta shape in my pantry.

—Mary Tallman Arbor Vitae, WI

Prep: 30 min. • **Cook:** 8 hours
Makes: 9 servings

- **1 pound ground beef**
- **1 pound bulk Italian sausage**
- **1 can (28 ounces) crushed tomatoes, undrained**
- **1 medium green pepper, chopped**
- **1 medium onion, chopped**
- **2 medium carrots, finely chopped**
- **1 cup water**
- **1 can (8 ounces) tomato sauce**
- **1 can (6 ounces) tomato paste**
- **1 tablespoon brown sugar**
- **1 tablespoon Italian seasoning**
- **2 garlic cloves, minced**
- **½ teaspoon salt**
- **¼ teaspoon pepper**
- **Hot cooked spaghetti**

1. In a large skillet, cook the beef and sausage over medium heat until no longer pink; drain.
2. Transfer to a 5-qt. slow cooker. Stir in the tomatoes, green pepper, onion, carrots, water, tomato sauce, tomato paste, brown sugar, Italian seasoning, garlic, salt and pepper. Cover and cook on low for 8-10 hours or until bubbly. Serve with spaghetti.
Freeze option: Do not cook spaghetti. Freeze meat sauce in freezer containers. To use, partially thaw in the refrigerator overnight. Cook spaghetti according to package directions. Place sauce in a large saucepan; heat through, stirring sauce occasionally and adding a little water if necessary. Serve over spaghetti.

FARM-STYLE BBQ RIBS

Inspiration struck when I saw a recipe like this one in a newspaper. My version was an instant hit with my husband and our friends. And then, when I discovered how to make it in the slow cooker, it got even better—and easier.

—Bette Jo Welton Eugene, OR

Prep: 20 min. • **Cook:** 6 hours
Makes: 4 servings

- **4 pounds bone-in beef short ribs**
- **1 can (15 ounces) thick and zesty tomato sauce**
- **1½ cups water**
- **1 medium onion, chopped**
- **1 can (6 ounces) tomato paste**
- **⅓ cup packed brown sugar**
- **3 tablespoons cider vinegar**
- **3 tablespoons Worcestershire sauce**
- **2 tablespoons chili powder**
- **4 garlic cloves, minced**
- **2 teaspoons ground mustard**
- **1½ teaspoons salt**

Place ribs in a 5- or 6-qt. slow cooker. In a large saucepan, combine the remaining ingredients. Bring to a boil. Reduce heat; simmer, uncovered, 5 minutes or until slightly thickened. Pour over ribs; cook, covered, on low 6-8 hours or until tender.

FARM-STYLE BBQ RIBS

MANGO-PINEAPPLE CHICKEN TACOS

I lived in the Caribbean as a child, and the fresh tropical fruits in this delectable chicken entree bring me back to those happy days.

—Lissa Nelson Provo, UT

Prep: 25 min. • **Cook:** 5 hours
Makes: 16 servings

- **2 medium mangoes, peeled and chopped**
- **1½ cups cubed fresh pineapple or canned pineapple chunks, drained**
- **2 medium tomatoes, chopped**
- **1 medium red onion, finely chopped**
- **2 small Anaheim peppers, seeded and chopped**
- **2 green onions, finely chopped**
- **1 tablespoon lime juice**
- **1 teaspoon sugar**
- **4 pounds bone-in chicken breast halves, skin removed**
- **3 teaspoons salt**
- **¼ cup packed brown sugar**
- **32 taco shells, warmed**
- **¼ cup minced fresh cilantro**

1. In a large bowl, combine the first eight ingredients. Place chicken in a 6-qt. slow cooker; sprinkle with salt and brown sugar. Top with mango mixture. Cover and cook on low for 5-6 hours or until chicken is tender.
2. Remove chicken; cool slightly. Strain cooking juices, reserving mango mixture and ½ cup juices. Discard the remaining juices. When cool enough to handle, remove chicken from bones; discard the bones.
3. Shred chicken with two forks. Return chicken and reserved mango mixture and cooking juices to slow cooker; heat through. Serve in taco shells; sprinkle with cilantro.

Freeze option: Freeze cooled meat mixture in freezer containers. To use, partially thaw in refrigerator overnight. Heat through in a saucepan, stirring occasionally and adding a little broth if necessary.

SEAFOOD CIOPPINO

If you're looking for a great seafood recipe for your slow cooker, this classic fish stew is just the ticket. It's brimming with clams, crab, fish and shrimp. It's easy, yet fancy enough to be an elegant meal.
—Lisa Moriarty Wilton, NH

Prep: 20 min. • **Cook:** 4½ hours
Makes: 8 servings (2½ quarts)

- **1 can (28 ounces) diced tomatoes, undrained**
- **2 medium onions, chopped**
- **3 celery ribs, chopped**
- **1 bottle (8 ounces) clam juice**
- **1 can (6 ounces) tomato paste**
- **½ cup white wine or ½ cup vegetable broth**
- **5 garlic cloves, minced**
- **1 tablespoon red wine vinegar**
- **1 tablespoon olive oil**
- **1 to 2 teaspoons Italian seasoning**
- **1 bay leaf**
- **½ teaspoon sugar**
- **1 pound haddock fillets, cut into 1-inch pieces**
- **1 pound uncooked shrimp (41-50 per pound), peeled and deveined**
- **1 can (6 ounces) chopped clams, undrained**
- **1 can (6 ounces) lump crabmeat, drained**
- **2 tablespoons minced fresh parsley**

1. In a 4- or 5-qt. slow cooker, combine the first 12 ingredients. Cook, covered, on low 4-5 hours.
2. Stir in seafood. Cook, covered, for 20-30 minutes longer or until the fish just begins to flake easily with a fork and the shrimp turn pink.
3. Remove bay leaf. Stir in parsley.

SLOW-COOKED PORK BURRITOS

I've been making this recipe for 20 years, changing it here and there. Now I serve this delicious version. It's become our favorite for casual summer get-togethers.
—Sharon Belmont Lincoln, NE

Prep: 20 min. • **Cook:** 8 hours
Makes: 14 servings

- **1 boneless pork sirloin roast (3 pounds)**
- **¼ cup reduced-sodium chicken broth**
- **1 envelope reduced-sodium taco seasoning**
- **1 tablespoon dried parsley flakes**
- **2 garlic cloves, minced**
- **½ teaspoon pepper**
- **¼ teaspoon salt**
- **1 can (16 ounces) refried beans**
- **1 can (4 ounces) chopped green chilies**
- **14 flour tortillas (8 inches), warmed**
- **Optional toppings: shredded lettuce, chopped tomatoes, chopped green pepper, guacamole, reduced-fat sour cream and shredded reduced-fat cheddar cheese**

1. Cut roast in half; place in a 4- or 5-qt. slow cooker. In a small bowl, mix broth, taco seasoning, parsley, garlic, pepper and salt; pour over roast. Cook, covered, on low for 8-10 hours or until the meat is very tender.
2. Remove pork from slow cooker; cool slightly. Shred meat with two forks. Skim fat from cooking juices. Return cooking juices and pork to slow cooker. Stir in beans and chilies; heat through.
3. Spoon ½ cup pork mixture across center of each tortilla; add toppings as desired. Fold bottom and sides of the tortilla over filling and roll up.

To freeze burritos: Roll up burritos without toppings. Wrap individually in paper towels, then foil. Transfer to a resealable plastic bag. May be frozen for up to 2 months. To use frozen burritos, remove foil. Place paper towel-wrapped burritos on a microwave-safe plate. Microwave on high for 3-4 minutes or until heated through. Serve with toppings as desired.

SLOW-COOKED PORK BURRITOS

GARDEN CHICKEN CACCIATORE

Treat company to this perfect Italian meal. You'll have time to visit with your guests while it simmers, and it often earns me rave reviews. I like to serve it with couscous, green beans and a dry red wine. Mangia!
—Martha Schirmacher
Sterling Heights, MI

Prep: 15 min. • **Cook:** 8½ hours
Makes: 12 servings

- **12 boneless skinless chicken thighs (about 3 pounds)**
- **2 medium green peppers, chopped**
- **1 can (14½ ounces) diced tomatoes with basil, oregano and garlic, undrained**
- **1 can (6 ounces) tomato paste**
- **1 medium onion, sliced**
- **½ cup reduced-sodium chicken broth**
- **¼ cup dry red wine or additional reduced-sodium chicken broth**
- **3 garlic cloves, minced**
- **¾ teaspoon salt**
- **⅛ teaspoon pepper**
- **2 tablespoons cornstarch**
- **2 tablespoons cold water**

1. Place chicken in a 4- or 5-qt. slow cooker. In a medium bowl, combine green peppers, tomatoes, tomato paste, onion, broth, wine, garlic, salt and pepper; pour over chicken. Cook, covered, on low 8-10 hours or until chicken is tender.
2. In a small bowl, mix cornstarch and water until smooth; gradually stir into slow cooker. Cook, covered, on high for 30 minutes or until sauce is thickened.

CAJUN PORK & RICE

I created this recipe upon returning home after traveling. With not much food in the house, I used the ingredients I had on hand, and my husband loved it. He loves the dish because it's tasty, and I love it because it's easy.

—Allison Gapinski Cary, NC

Prep: 20 min. • **Cook:** 4 hours 10 min.
Makes: 4 servings

- **1½ teaspoons ground cumin**
- **1½ teaspoons chili powder**
- **1½ pounds boneless pork loin chops**
- **1 can (14½ ounces) petite diced tomatoes, undrained**
- **1 small onion, finely chopped**
- **1 celery rib, finely chopped**
- **1 small carrot, julienned**
- **1 garlic clove, minced**
- **½ teaspoon Louisiana-style hot sauce**
- **¼ teaspoon salt**
- **1½ cups uncooked instant rice**
- **1 cup reduced-sodium chicken broth**
- **1 teaspoon olive oil**
- **1 medium green pepper, julienned**

1. Mix cumin and chili powder; sprinkle pork chops with 2 teaspoon spice mixture. Transfer to a 4-qt. slow cooker.
2. In a small bowl, mix tomatoes, onion, celery, carrot, garlic, hot sauce, salt and remaining spice mixture; pour over the chops. Cook, covered, on low 4-5 hours or until meat is tender.
3. Stir in rice and chicken broth, breaking up pork into pieces. Cook, covered, on low 10-15 minutes longer or until rice is tender. In a small skillet, heat oil over medium-high heat. Add green pepper; cook and stir for 5-7 minutes or until crisp-tender. Serve with pork mixture.

(5) INGREDIENTS

SECRET'S IN THE SAUCE BBQ RIBS

Slow cooking makes these ribs so tender that the meat literally falls off the bones. And the sweet, rich sauce is simply wonderful. Yum!

—Tanya Reid Winston Salem, NC

Prep: 10 min. • **Cook:** 6 hours
Makes: 5 servings

- **4½ pounds pork baby back ribs**
- **1½ teaspoons pepper**
- **2½ cups barbecue sauce**
- **¾ cup cherry preserves**
- **1 tablespoon Dijon mustard**
- **1 garlic clove, minced**

Cut ribs into serving-size pieces; sprinkle with pepper. Place in a 5- or 6-qt. slow cooker. Combine remaining ingredients; pour over ribs. Cover and cook on low for 6-8 hours or until meat is tender. Serve with sauce.

TOMATO-TOPPED ITALIAN PORK CHOPS

Time to bring out the slow cooker! You're only seven ingredients away from a really delicious meal.

—Krystle Chasse Radium Hot Springs, BC

Prep: 25 min. • **Cook:** 8 hours
Makes: 6 servings

- **6 bone-in pork loin chops (7 ounces each)**
- **1 tablespoon canola oil**
- **1 small onion, chopped**
- **½ cup chopped carrot**
- **1 can (14½ ounces) diced tomatoes, drained**
- **¼ cup reduced-fat balsamic vinaigrette**
- **2 teaspoons dried oregano**

1. In a large skillet, brown chops in oil in batches. Transfer to a 4- or 5-qt. slow cooker coated with cooking spray. Saute onion and carrot in drippings until tender. Stir in the tomatoes, vinaigrette and oregano; pour over chops.
2. Cover and cook on low for 8-10 hours or until meat is tender.

SECRET'S IN THE SAUCE BBQ RIBS

FLAVORFUL LEMON CHICKEN

This easy and attractive meal is bound to become a staple in your home. Made with everyday ingredients, there's nothing complicated or fancy about this great find—just down-home goodness.

—Elizabeth Hokanson Arborg, MB

Prep: 20 min. • **Cook:** 4¼ hours
Makes: 6 servings

- **1 teaspoon dried oregano**
- **½ teaspoon seasoned salt**
- **¼ teaspoon pepper**
- **6 boneless skinless chicken breast halves (6 ounces each)**
- **2 teaspoons chicken bouillon granules**
- **¼ cup boiling water**
- **3 tablespoons lemon juice**
- **1½ teaspoons minced garlic**
- **1½ cups (12 ounces) sour cream**
- **2 teaspoons minced fresh parsley**
- **Hot cooked brown rice, optional**

1. Combine the oregano, seasoned salt and pepper; rub over chicken. Place in a 3-qt. slow cooker.
2. In a small bowl, dissolve bouillon in boiling water. Stir in lemon juice and garlic. Pour over chicken. Cover and cook on low for 4-5 hours or until chicken the is tender.
3. Remove chicken and keep warm. Stir in sour cream and parsley; cover and cook for 15 minutes or until heated through. Serve chicken with sauce and, if desired, rice.

★★★★★ **READER REVIEW**

"Delicious! The chicken was moist, tender and full of flavor. The lemon called for was just enough, and it was not overwhelming. In fact, the sauce was great with the chicken, and it enhanced the nutty flavor of the brown rice. This recipe is a keeper."

ROSOMALLEY TASTEOFHOME.COM

TOMATO-BASIL STEAK

I use basil and bell peppers from my herb and vegetable garden to make this main course. It's so easy to prepare and so savory and delicious.

—Sherry Little Sherwood, AR

Prep: 15 min. • **Cook:** 6 hours
Makes: 4 servings

- **1¼ pounds boneless beef shoulder top blade or flat iron steaks**
- **½ pound whole fresh mushrooms, quartered**
- **1 medium sweet yellow pepper, julienned**
- **1 can (14½ ounces) stewed tomatoes, undrained**
- **1 can (8 ounces) tomato sauce**
- **1 envelope onion soup mix**
- **2 tablespoons minced fresh basil**
- **Hot cooked rice**

1. Place steaks in a 4-qt. slow cooker. Add mushrooms and pepper. In a small bowl, mix tomatoes, tomato sauce, soup mix and basil; pour over top.
2. Cook, covered, on low 6-8 hours or until beef and vegetables are tender. Serve with rice.

MOM'S SCALLOPED POTATOES & HAM

My mom's friend gave her this recipe years ago, and she shared it with me. When we have leftover ham to use up, it's the most-requested dish at my house.

—Kelly Graham St. Thomas, ON

Prep: 20 min. • **Cook:** 8 hours
Makes: 9 servings

- **10 medium potatoes (about 3 pounds), peeled and thinly sliced**
- **3 cups cubed fully cooked ham**
- **2 large onions, thinly sliced**
- **2 cups shredded cheddar cheese**
- **1 can (10¾ ounces) condensed cream of mushroom soup, undiluted**
- **½ teaspoon paprika**
- **¼ teaspoon pepper**

1. In a greased 6-qt. slow cooker, layer half of the potatoes, ham, onions and cheese. Repeat layers. Pour soup over top. Sprinkle with paprika and pepper.
2. Cover and cook on low for 8-10 hours or until potatoes are tender.

TOMATO-BASIL STEAK

LEMON DILL CHICKEN

LEMON DILL CHICKEN

The lemon and dill in this recipe give the chicken a bright, fresh taste. Pair the entree with a loaf of bread and a mixed green salad.

—**Lori Lockrey** Pickering, ON

Prep: 20 min. • **Cook:** 4 hours + standing
Makes: 6 servings

- **2 medium onions, coarsely chopped**
- **2 tablespoons butter, softened**
- **¼ teaspoon grated lemon peel**
- **1 broiler/fryer chicken (4 to 5 pounds)**
- **¼ cup chicken stock**
- **4 sprigs fresh parsley**
- **4 fresh dill sprigs**
- **3 tablespoons lemon juice**
- **1 teaspoon salt**
- **1 teaspoon paprika**
- **½ teaspoon dried thyme**
- **¼ teaspoon pepper**

1. Place onions on bottom of a 6-qt. slow cooker. In a small bowl, mix butter and lemon peel.
2. Tuck wings under the chicken; tie drumsticks together. With your fingers, carefully loosen skin from chicken breast; rub butter mixture under the skin. Secure skin to the underside of the breast with toothpicks. Place chicken over onions, breast side up. Add stock, parsley and dill.
3. Drizzle lemon juice over chicken; sprinkle with seasonings. Cook, covered, on low for 4-5 hours (a thermometer inserted in chicken thigh should read at least 170°).
4. Remove chicken from slow cooker; tent with foil. Let stand for 15 minutes before carving.

DELUXE
WALKING
NACHOS

DELUXE WALKING NACHOS

This slow-cooked potluck chili makes an awesome filling for a bag of walk-around nachos. Cut the bag lengthwise to make it easier to load up your fork.

—Mallory Lynch Madison, WI

Prep: 20 min. • **Cook:** 6 hours
Makes: 18 servings

- **1 pound lean ground beef (90% lean)**
- **1 large sweet onion, chopped**
- **3 garlic cloves, minced**
- **2 cans (14½ ounces each) diced tomatoes with mild green chilies**
- **2 cans (15 ounces each) pinto beans, rinsed and drained**
- **2 cans (15 ounces each) black beans, rinsed and drained**
- **2 to 3 tablespoons chili powder**
- **2 teaspoons ground cumin**
- **½ teaspoon salt**
- **18 packages (1 ounce each) nacho-flavored tortilla chips**
- **Optional toppings: shredded cheddar cheese, sour cream, chopped tomatoes and pickled jalapeno slices**

1. In a large skillet, cook beef, onion and garlic over medium heat 6-8 minutes or until beef is no longer pink, breaking up beef into crumbles; drain.
2. Transfer the beef mixture to a 5-qt. slow cooker. Drain one can tomatoes, discarding liquid; add to slow cooker. Stir in beans, chili powder, cumin, salt and remaining tomatoes. Cook, covered, on low 6-8 hours to allow flavors to blend. Mash beans to desired consistency.
3. Just before serving, cut open tortilla chip bags. Divide chili among bags; add toppings as desired.

Freeze option: Freeze cooled chili in a freezer container. To use, partially thaw in refrigerator overnight. Heat through in a saucepan, stirring occasionally and adding a little water if necessary.

SLOW COOKER CURRY CHICKEN

SLOW COOKER CURRY CHICKEN

My husband travels for business and discovered that he likes Indian cuisine. This simple slow-cooked recipe delivers those delicious curry flavors. Use some parsley if you don't have cilantro.

—Katie Schultz Temple, GA

Prep: 15 min. • **Cook:** 3 hours
Makes: 4 servings

- **2 medium onions, cut into wedges**
- **2 medium sweet red peppers, cut into 1-inch strips**
- **4 boneless skinless chicken breast halves (6 ounces each)**
- **2 tablespoons curry powder, divided**
- **1 teaspoon salt, divided**
- **1 cup light coconut milk**
- **½ cup chicken broth**
- **3 garlic cloves, minced**
- **½ teaspoon pepper**
- **1 cup chopped dried apricots (about 6 ounces)**
- **Hot cooked rice and lime wedges**
- **Chopped cashews and minced fresh cilantro, optional**

1. Place onions and peppers in a 4-qt. slow cooker. Sprinkle chicken with 1 tablespoon curry powder and ½ teaspoon salt; place over vegetables.
2. In a small bowl, whisk coconut milk, broth, garlic, pepper and the remaining curry powder and salt. Pour into slow cooker. Cook, covered, on low for 3-3½ hours or until the chicken is tender (a thermometer should read at least 165°), adding apricots during the last 30 minutes of cooking.
3. Serve with rice and lime wedges. If desired, sprinkle curry with cashews and cilantro.

SWEET ONION CREAMED CORN

SIDE DISHES

Beat the heat when you let your slow cooker simmer a side dish to bubbly perfection. These tasty options keep the kitchen cool, save oven space and transport easily!

SWEET ONION CREAMED CORN

A friend from church gave me this delicious, easy recipe more than 40 years ago, and I still make it regularly. She was from the South, and whenever I cook it, I think about her fondly.

—**Nancy Heishman** Las Vegas, NV

Prep: 25 min. • **Cook:** 3 hours
Makes: 8 servings

- **5 bacon strips, chopped**
- **1 large sweet onion, chopped**
- **1 medium sweet red pepper, chopped**
- **5 cups frozen corn (about 24 ounces), thawed**
- **2 cups cubed fully cooked ham**
- **½ cup half-and-half cream**
- **1 tablespoon brown sugar**
- **1 tablespoon dried parsley flakes**
- **1 teaspoon smoked paprika**
- **½ teaspoon salt**
- **½ teaspoon pepper**
- **1 package (8 ounces) cream cheese, cubed and softened**

1. In a large skillet, cook bacon over medium heat until crisp, stirring occasionally. Remove with a slotted spoon; drain on paper towels.
2. Cook and stir onion and sweet red pepper in bacon drippings over medium-high heat until tender, 5-6 minutes.
3. In a greased 4-qt. slow cooker, combine corn, ham, cream, brown sugar, parsley, paprika, salt, pepper, bacon and onion mixture. Cook, covered, on low until heated through, 3-4 hours. Stir in cream cheese; cook, covered, 10 minutes longer. Stir before serving.

SLOW-COOKED CHEESY POTATOES

For a comforting side dish that feeds a crowd, try these saucy potatoes. A simple topping of buttered croutons covers the creamy combination quickly and easily.

—**Melissa Marzolf** Marysville, MI

Prep: 10 min. • **Cook:** 8 hours
Makes: 12 servings

- **6 medium potatoes, peeled and cut into ¼-inch strips**
- **2 cups shredded cheddar cheese**
- **1 can (10¾ ounces) condensed cream of chicken soup, undiluted**
- **1 small onion, chopped or 1 tablespoon dried minced onion**
- **7 tablespoons butter, melted, divided**
- **1 teaspoon salt**
- **1 teaspoon pepper**
- **1 cup (8 ounces) sour cream**
- **2 cups seasoned stuffing cubes**

1. Toss the potatoes and cheese; place in a 5-qt. slow cooker. Combine the soup, onion, 4 tablespoons butter, salt and pepper; pour over the potato mixture.
2. Cover and cook on low for 8-10 hours or until potatoes are tender. Stir in sour cream. Toss stuffing cubes and remaining butter; sprinkle over potatoes.

★★★★★ **READER REVIEW**

"Very yummy! I made this potato side dish in the oven instead and cooked it for about 1 hour at 350°."

AMESREIP TASTEOFHOME.COM

GLAZED SPICED CARROTS

Glazed carrots are a classic side dish for special occasions. This side is easy to put together, and people really enjoy it.
—*Taste of Home* Test Kitchen

Prep: 10 min. • **Cook:** 6 hours
Makes: 6 servings

2 pounds small carrots
½ cup peach preserves
½ cup butter, melted
¼ cup packed brown sugar
1 teaspoon vanilla extract
½ teaspoon ground cinnamon
¼ teaspoon salt
⅛ teaspoon ground nutmeg
2 tablespoons cornstarch
2 tablespoons water
Toasted chopped pecans, optional

1. Place carrots in a 3-qt. slow cooker. Combine the preserves, butter, brown sugar, vanilla, cinnamon, salt and nutmeg. Combine cornstarch and water until smooth; stir into preserve mixture. Pour over carrots.
2. Cover and cook on low for 6-8 hours or until tender. Stir carrots; sprinkle with pecans if desired.

Note: To toast nuts, bake in a shallow pan in a 350° oven for 5-10 minutes or cook nuts in a skillet over low heat until lightly browned, stirring occasionally.

CREAMED CORN

(5) INGREDIENTS

CREAMED CORN

Five ingredients are all you'll need for my popular dinner accompaniment. It's wonderful no matter what the occasion. Try it at your next barbecue, for sloppy-joe night or even in a holiday menu.
—Barbara Brizendine Harrisonville, MO

Prep: 10 min. • **Cook:** 3 hours
Makes: 5 servings

2 packages (one 16 ounces, one 10 ounces) frozen corn
1 package (8 ounces) cream cheese, softened and cubed
¼ cup butter, cubed
1 tablespoon sugar
½ teaspoon salt

In a 3-qt. slow cooker coated with cooking spray, combine all ingredients. Cover and cook on low for 3 to 3½ hours or until cheese is melted and corn is tender. Stir just before serving.

DID YOU KNOW?

When using a slow cooker, make sure you cube certain ingredients. Cream cheese and other brick cheeses, for instance, will melt faster and combine more evenly with other ingredients when cubed before being added to the slow cooker.

(5) INGREDIENTS

EASY BEANS & POTATOES WITH BACON

I love the combination of green beans with bacon, so I created this recipe. It's great when you have company because you can start it in the slow cooker and then later continue preparing the rest of your dinner.

—**Barbara Brittain** Santee, CA

Prep: 15 min. • **Cook:** 6 hours
Makes: 10 servings

- **8 bacon strips, chopped**
- **1½ pounds fresh green beans, trimmed and cut into 2-inch pieces (about 4 cups)**
- **4 medium potatoes, peeled and cut into ½-inch cubes**
- **1 small onion, halved and sliced**
- **¼ cup reduced-sodium chicken broth**
- **½ teaspoon salt**
- **¼ teaspoon pepper**

1. In a large skillet, cook bacon over medium heat until crisp, stirring occasionally. Remove to paper towels with a slotted spoon; drain, reserving 1 tablespoon drippings. Cover and refrigerate bacon until serving.
2. In a 5-qt. slow cooker, combine the remaining ingredients; stir in reserved drippings. Cover and cook on low for 6-8 hours or until potatoes are tender. Stir in bacon; heat through.

EASY BEANS & POTATOES WITH BACON

VEGETABLE MEDLEY

Here's a wonderful side dish to make when garden vegetables are plentiful. If you have fresh corn, use that instead of frozen. It will complement any summer entree you have in mind.

—**Terry Maly** Olathe, KS

Prep: 15 min. • **Cook:** 5 hours
Makes: 8 servings

- **4 cups diced peeled potatoes**
- **1½ cups frozen whole kernel corn**
- **4 medium tomatoes, seeded and diced**
- **1 cup sliced carrots**
- **½ cup chopped onion**
- **¾ teaspoon salt**
- **½ teaspoon sugar**
- **½ teaspoon dill weed**
- **⅛ teaspoon pepper**

In a 3-qt. slow cooker, combine all ingredients. Cover and cook on low for 5-6 hours or until vegetables are tender.

SLOW-COOKED RATATOUILLE

SLOW-COOKED RATATOUILLE

I get my son to eat eggplant by cooking it low and slow in this classic French veggie dish. Serve it as a meatless main with a side of rice and bread.

—**Diane Goedde** Red Lodge, MT

Prep: 25 min. + standing • **Cook:** 5 hours
Makes: 10 servings

- **1 medium eggplant, peeled and cut into 1-inch cubes**
- **1 tablespoon plus 1 teaspoon salt, divided**
- **2 medium onions, halved and thinly sliced**
- **4 medium tomatoes, chopped**
- **3 medium zucchini, cut into ¾-inch slices**
- **2 celery ribs, chopped**
- **3 tablespoons olive oil**
- **2 teaspoons dried basil or 2 tablespoons minced fresh basil**
- **4 garlic cloves, minced**
- **½ teaspoon pepper**
- **1 can (6 ounces) tomato paste**
- **1 can (2¼ ounces) sliced ripe olives, drained**
- **⅓ cup coarsely chopped fresh basil**

1. Place eggplant in a colander over a plate; sprinkle with 1 tablespoon salt and toss. Let stand 45 minutes. Rinse and drain well; blot dry with paper towels.
2. Place eggplant and remaining vegetables in a 5- or 6-qt. slow cooker. Add oil, dried basil, garlic, pepper and remaining salt; toss to combine.
3. Cook, covered, on low 5-6 hours or until onions are tender. Stir in tomato paste, olives and fresh basil; heat the ratatouille through.

Freeze option: Freeze cooled ratatouille in freezer containers. To use, partially thaw in refrigerator overnight. Microwave, covered, on high in a microwave-safe dish until heated through, stirring gently.

★★★★★ **READER REVIEW**

"This is delicious! I served it on pasta with garlic bread on the side. Yum!"

BROOKE TASTEOFHOME.COM

BLACK BEAN POTATO AU GRATIN

The addition of black beans and vegetables add both protein and fiber to this dinner add-on. And for a southwestern twist, you can try adding a handful or two of chopped cooked ham or chorizo sausage; replace the peas with one cup of corn.

—Erin Chilcoat Central Islip, NY

Prep: 25 min. • **Cook:** 8 hours
Makes: 6 servings

- **2 cans (15 ounces each) black beans, rinsed and drained**
- **1 can (10¾ ounces) condensed cream of mushroom soup, undiluted**
- **1 medium sweet red pepper, chopped**
- **1 cup frozen peas**
- **1 cup chopped sweet onion**
- **1 celery rib, thinly sliced**
- **2 garlic cloves, minced**
- **1 teaspoon dried thyme**
- **¼ teaspoon coarsely ground pepper**
- **1½ pounds medium red potatoes, cut into ¼-inch slices**
- **1 teaspoon salt**
- **1 cup shredded cheddar cheese**

In a bowl, combine the beans, soup, red pepper, peas, onion, celery, garlic, thyme and pepper. Spoon half of mixture into a greased 3- or 4-qt. slow cooker. Layer with half of the potatoes, salt and cheese. Repeat layers. Cover and cook on low for 8-10 hours or until potatoes are tender.

BLACK BEAN POTATO AU GRATIN

GREEN BEANS & NEW POTATOES

The beans and potatoes come out tender in this side dish, and the onion soup mix and onion add lots of flavor to the broth.

—Ann Baker Texarkana, TX

Prep: 15 min. • **Cook:** 6 hours
Makes: 10 servings

- **1 pound fresh green beans, trimmed**
- **1 pound small red potatoes, quartered**
- **½ pound medium fresh mushrooms, halved**
- **½ cup thinly sliced sweet onion**
- **2 cans (14½ ounces each) beef broth**
- **2 tablespoons beefy onion soup mix**
- **2 teaspoons Worcestershire sauce**
- **1 teaspoon grated lemon peel**
- **½ teaspoon salt**
- **½ teaspoon pepper**
- **¼ teaspoon garlic powder**

In a 5-qt. slow cooker, layer the green beans, potatoes, mushrooms and onion. In a small bowl, combine the remaining ingredients; pour over vegetables. Cover and cook on low for 6-8 hours or until vegetables are tender. Serve with a slotted spoon.

ITALIAN MUSHROOMS

5 INGREDIENTS

ITALIAN MUSHROOMS

Only four ingredients create a rich and flavorful side dish that we love to eat with beef and mashed potatoes.

—Kim Reichert Fargo, ND

Prep: 10 min. • **Cook:** 4 hours
Makes: 6 servings

- **1 pound medium fresh mushrooms**
- **1 large onion, sliced**
- **½ cup butter, melted**
- **1 envelope Italian salad dressing mix**

In a 3-qt. slow cooker, layer mushrooms and onion. Combine butter and salad dressing mix; pour over vegetables. Cover and cook on low for 4-5 hours or until vegetables are tender. Serve with a slotted spoon.

SLOW-COOKED SUMMER SQUASH

We love squash but I got tired of fixing it the usual way...with a little cheese. I decided to jazz things up a bit, and here is the result. It's a huge hit with the family!

—Joan Hallford North Richland Hills, TX

Prep: 15 min. • **Cook:** 2 hours
Makes: 8 servings

- **1 pound medium yellow summer squash**
- **1 pound medium zucchini**
- **2 medium tomatoes, chopped**
- **¼ cup thinly sliced green onions**
- **½ teaspoon salt**
- **¼ teaspoon pepper**
- **1 cup vegetable broth**
- **1½ cups Caesar salad croutons, coarsely crushed**
- **½ cup shredded cheddar cheese**
- **4 bacon strips, cooked and crumbled**

1. Cut yellow squash and zucchini into ¼-in.-thick slices. In a 3- or 4-qt. slow cooker, combine the squash, tomatoes and green onions. Add salt and pepper; pour in broth. Cook, covered, on low until tender, 2½-3½ hours. Remove with a slotted spoon; drain well.
2. To serve, sprinkle with croutons, cheese and bacon.

SLOW COOKER BBQ BAKED BEANS

SLOW COOKER BBQ BAKED BEANS

I was under doctor's orders to reduce sodium, but I just couldn't part with some of my all-time favorite foods. After many experiments I came up with this potluck pleaser—now everyone's happy!

—Sherrel Hendrix Arkadelphia, AR

Prep: 10 min. + soaking
Cook: 8½ hours
Makes: 12 servings (½ cup each)

- **1 package (16 ounces) dried great northern beans**
- **2 smoked ham hocks (about ½ pound each)**
- **2 cups water**
- **1 medium onion, chopped**
- **2 teaspoons garlic powder, divided**
- **2 teaspoons onion powder, divided**
- **1 cup barbecue sauce**
- **¾ cup packed brown sugar**
- **½ teaspoon ground nutmeg**
- **¼ teaspoon ground cloves**
- **2 teaspoons hot pepper sauce, optional**

1. Rinse and sort beans; soak according to package directions. Drain and rinse beans, discarding liquid.
2. In a 4-qt. slow cooker, combine beans, ham hocks, water, onion, 1 teaspoon garlic powder and 1 teaspoon onion powder. Cook, covered, on low until beans are tender, 8-10 hours.
3. Remove ham hocks; cool slightly. Cut meat into small cubes, discarding bones; return meat to slow cooker. Stir in the barbecue sauce, brown sugar, nutmeg, cloves, remaining garlic powder, remaining onion powder and, if desired, pepper sauce. Cook, covered, on high until heated through, about 30 minutes.

TEST KITCHEN TIP

Using hot sauce to flavor foods can be a smart alternative to salt, but make sure you check the nutrition labels. We recommend Tabasco sauce. It has only 26mg of sodium per 5-7 drops.

CHEESY SPINACH

CHEESY SPINACH

My daughter often serves this cheese-spinach blend at church suppers. Even people who don't usually eat spinach like this flavorful dish once they try it. There is never any left.

—Frances Moore Decatur, IL

Prep: 10 min. • **Cook:** 5 hours
Makes: 8 servings

- **2 packages (10 ounces each) frozen chopped spinach, thawed and well drained**
- **2 cups (16 ounces) 4% cottage cheese**
- **1½ cups cubed process cheese (Velveeta)**
- **3 large eggs, lightly beaten**
- **¼ cup butter, cubed**
- **¼ cup all-purpose flour**
- **1 teaspoon salt**

In a large bowl, combine all ingredients. Pour into a greased 3-qt. slow cooker. Cover and cook on high for 1 hour. Reduce heat to low; cook 4-5 hours longer or until a knife inserted in the center comes out clean.

HASH BROWNS WITH HAM

Convenient grocery store items like frozen hash browns and a can of chicken soup make this an easy-to-make dish. Both kids and adults love it because it's super tasty and chock-full of cheese.

—Lightningbug *Taste of Home.com*

Prep: 15 min. • **Cook:** 3¼ hours
Makes: 8 servings

- **1 package (32 ounces) frozen cubed hash brown potatoes, thawed**
- **1 cup cubed fully cooked ham**
- **1 small onion, chopped**
- **2 cups shredded cheddar cheese, divided**
- **1 can (14¾ ounces) condensed cream of chicken soup, undiluted**
- **½ cup butter, melted**
- **1 cup (8 ounces) sour cream**

1. In a 3-qt. slow cooker, combine the potatoes, ham, onion and 1 cup cheese. Combine soup and butter; pour over potato mixture. Cover and cook on low for 3-4 hours or until the potatoes are tender.
2. Stir in sour cream. Sprinkle with remaining cheese. Cover and cook mixture for 15 minutes or until the cheese is melted.

POTLUCK MACARONI & CHEESE

Here's a no-fuss way to make America's most popular comfort food. The dish turns out cheesy, rich and extra creamy.
—Jennifer Babcock Chicopee, MA

Prep: 25 min. • **Cook:** 2 hours
Makes: 16 servings (¾ cup each)

- **3 cups uncooked elbow macaroni**
- **1 package (16 ounces) process cheese (Velveeta), cubed**
- **2 cups shredded Mexican cheese blend**
- **2 cups shredded white cheddar cheese**
- **1¾ cups whole milk**
- **1 can (12 ounces) evaporated milk**
- **¾ cup butter, melted**
- **3 large eggs, lightly beaten**

1. Cook macaroni according to package directions for al dente; drain. Transfer to a greased 5-qt. slow cooker. Stir in the remaining ingredients.
2. Cook mixture, covered, on low until a thermometer reads at least 160°, 2-2½ hours, stirring once.

POTLUCK MACARONI & CHEESE

(5) INGREDIENTS

LEMON RED POTATOES

Butter, lemon juice, parsley and chives enhance this simple side dish. I usually prepare these potatoes when I'm having company. Since they cook in the slow cooker, there's plenty of room on the stove for other dishes.
—Tara Branham Austin, TX

Prep: 5 min. • **Cook:** 2½ hours
Makes: 6 servings

- **1½ pounds medium red potatoes**
- **¼ cup water**
- **¼ cup butter, melted**
- **3 tablespoons minced fresh parsley**
- **1 tablespoon lemon juice**
- **1 tablespoon minced chives**
- **Salt and pepper to taste**

1. Cut a strip of peel from around the middle of each potato. Place potatoes and water in a 3-qt. slow cooker. Cover and cook on high for 2½-3 hours or until tender (do not overcook); drain.
2. In a small bowl, combine the butter, parsley, lemon juice and chives. Pour over the potatoes and toss to coat. Season with salt and pepper.

TEST KITCHEN TIP

This potato recipe is versatile and works with many herbs and dried seasonings. Make up your own combination if you'd like!

SLOW COOKER SRIRACHA CORN

A restaurant here had been advertising Sriracha corn on the cob, but I knew I could make my own. The golden ears turned out a little sweet, a little smoky and a little hot—perfect, if you ask my three teenage boys!
—Julie Peterson Crofton, MD

Prep: 15 min. • **Cook:** 3 hours
Makes: 8 servings

- **½ cup butter, softened**
- **2 tablespoons honey**
- **1 tablespoon Sriracha Asian hot chili sauce**
- **1 teaspoon smoked paprika**
- **½ teaspoon kosher salt**
- **8 small ears sweet corn, husks removed**
- **¼ cup water**
- **Additional smoked paprika, optional**

1. Mix first five ingredients. Place each ear of corn on a 12x12-in. piece of heavy-duty foil; spread with 1 tablespoon butter mixture. Wrap the foil around corn, sealing tightly. Place in a 6-qt. slow cooker.
2. Add water; cook, covered, on low until corn is tender, 3-4 hours. If desired, sprinkle corn with additional paprika before serving.

SLOW COOKER SRIRACHA CORN

(5) INGREDIENTS
CHEDDAR SPIRALS

Our kids just love this cheesy pasta and will sample a spoonful right from the slow cooker when they walk by. Sometimes I add cocktail sausages, sliced Polish sausage or cubed ham to make it into a hearty main course.
—Heidi Ferkovich Park Falls, WI

Prep: 20 min. • **Cook:** 2½ hours
Makes: 15 servings (¾ cup each)

- **1 package (16 ounces) spiral pasta**
- **2 cups half-and-half cream**
- **1 can (10¾ ounces) condensed cheddar cheese soup, undiluted**
- **½ cup butter, melted**
- **4 cups shredded cheddar cheese**

Cook pasta according to package directions; drain. In a 5-qt. slow cooker, combine the cream, soup and butter until smooth; stir in the cheese and pasta. Cover and cook on low for 2½ hours or until cheese is melted.

SLOW-COOKED LEMONY SPRING VEGGIES

SLOW-COOKED LEMONY SPRING VEGGIES

These spuds do a slow simmer with carrots and onion for a comfort side that bucks up any entree. Finish with a sprinkle of fresh chives from the garden.
—*Taste of Home* Test Kitchen

Prep: 10 min. • **Cook:** 4¼ hours
Makes: 8 servings

- **4 medium carrots, halved lengthwise and cut into 1-inch pieces**
- **1 large sweet onion, coarsely chopped**
- **1½ pounds baby red potatoes, quartered**
- **3 tablespoons butter, melted**
- **¾ teaspoon salt**
- **¼ teaspoon pepper**
- **1 cup frozen peas, thawed**
- **1 teaspoon grated lemon zest**
- **¼ cup minced fresh chives**

1. Place carrots and onion in a 4-qt. slow cooker; top with potatoes. Drizzle with melted butter; sprinkle with salt and pepper. Cook, covered, on low 4-5 hours or until vegetables are tender.
2. Add peas to the slow cooker. Cook, covered, on high 10-15 minutes or until heated through. Stir in the lemon zest. Sprinkle with chives.

DID YOU KNOW?

Red potatoes are ideal for slow-cooked dishes because they hold their shape well, yet offer a terrifically tender flesh even when they undergo long cooking times. For the same reason, they're a better choice to boil for potato salads or in soups and stews.

PARSLEY SMASHED POTATOES

CORN SPOON BREAD

My spoon bread is moister than corn pudding made in the oven, and the cream cheese is a nice addition. It goes great with everything from grilled chicken to Christmas ham.

—Tamara Ellefson Frederic, WI

Prep: 15 min. • **Cook:** 3 hours
Makes: 8 servings

- **1 package (8 ounces) cream cheese, softened**
- **⅓ cup sugar**
- **1 cup 2% milk**
- **2 large eggs**
- **2 tablespoons butter, melted**
- **1 teaspoon salt**
- **¼ teaspoon ground nutmeg**
- **Dash pepper**
- **2⅓ cups frozen corn, thawed**
- **1 can (14¾ ounces) cream-style corn**
- **1 package (8½ ounces) corn bread/muffin mix**

1. In a large bowl, beat cream cheese and sugar until smooth. Gradually beat in milk. Beat in eggs, butter, salt, nutmeg and pepper until blended. Stir in corn and cream-style corn. Stir in corn bread mix just until moistened.
2. Pour into a greased 3-qt. slow cooker. Cover and cook on high for 3-4 hours or until center is almost set.

★★★★★ **READER REVIEW**

"I just made this for my mom's birthday dinner, and it instantly became our new favorite recipe. The flavors are well balanced (not too sweet or salty), and the corn bread and cream cheese make it a rich and savory textured mouthful."

MUZKLVR TASTEOFHOME.COM

PARSLEY SMASHED POTATOES

I love potatoes but hate the work involved in making mashed potatoes from scratch. So I came up with a simple side dish that was made even easier thanks to my slow cooker. Save the leftover broth for soup the next day!

—Katie Hagy Blacksburg, SC

Prep: 20 min. • **Cook:** 6 hours
Makes: 8 servings

- **16 small red potatoes (about 2 pounds)**
- **1 celery rib, sliced**
- **1 medium carrot, sliced**
- **¼ cup finely chopped onion**
- **2 cups chicken broth**
- **1 tablespoon minced fresh parsley**
- **1½ teaspoons salt, divided**
- **1 teaspoon pepper, divided**
- **1 garlic clove, minced**
- **2 tablespoons butter, melted**
- **Additional minced fresh parsley**

1. Place potatoes, celery, carrot and onion in a 4-qt. slow cooker. In a small bowl, mix broth, parsley, 1 teaspoon salt, ½ teaspoon pepper and garlic; pour over vegetables. Cook, covered, on low 6-8 hours or until potatoes are tender.
2. Transfer potatoes from slow cooker to a 15x10x1-in. pan; discard cooking liquid and vegetables. Using the bottom of a measuring cup, flatten the potatoes only slightly.
3. Transfer to a large bowl; drizzle with butter. Sprinkle with remaining salt and pepper; toss to coat. Sprinkle with additional parsley.

CORN SPOON BREAD

SLOW-COOKED BEAN MEDLEY

I often change the variety of beans in this classic recipe, using whatever I have on hand to a total of five 15- to 16-ounce cans. The sauce makes any combination delicious! It's a gluten-free side dish that's popular with just about everyone. Add it to your summer barbecues.

—**Peggy Gwillim** Strasbourg, , SK

Prep: 25 min. • **Cook:** 5 hours
Makes: 12 servings (¾ cup each)

- **1½ cups ketchup**
- **2 celery ribs, chopped**
- **1 medium onion, chopped**
- **1 medium green pepper, chopped**
- **1 medium sweet red pepper, chopped**
- **½ cup packed brown sugar**
- **½ cup water**
- **½ cup Italian salad dressing**
- **2 bay leaves**
- **1 tablespoon cider vinegar**
- **1 teaspoon ground mustard**
- **⅛ teaspoon pepper**
- **1 can (16 ounces) kidney beans, rinsed and drained**
- **1 can (15½ ounces) black-eyed peas, rinsed and drained**
- **1 can (15½ ounces) great northern beans, rinsed and drained**
- **1 can (15¼ ounces) whole kernel corn, drained**
- **1 can (15¼ ounces) lima beans, rinsed and drained**
- **1 can (15 ounces) black beans, rinsed and drained**

In a 5-qt. slow cooker, combine the first 12 ingredients. Stir in the remaining ingredients. Cover and cook on low for 5-6 hours or until onion and peppers are tender. Discard bay leaves.

BROCCOLI & CHEESE

BROCCOLI & CHEESE

This crumb-topped side dish is quick to assemble and full of flavor. Because it simmers in a slow cooker, it frees up my oven for other things. This is a big help when I'm preparing several items for a big meal at home.

—**Connie Slocum** Antioch, TN

Prep: 10 min. • **Cook:** 2¾ hours
Makes: 10 servings

- **6 cups frozen chopped broccoli, partially thawed**
- **1 can (10¾ ounces) condensed cream of celery soup, undiluted**
- **1½ cups shredded sharp cheddar cheese, divided**
- **¼ cup chopped onion**
- **½ teaspoon Worcestershire sauce**
- **¼ teaspoon pepper**
- **1 cup crushed butter-flavored crackers (about 25)**
- **2 tablespoons butter**

1. In a large bowl, combine the broccoli, celery soup, 1 cup cheese, onion, Worcestershire sauce and pepper. Pour into a greased 3-qt. slow cooker. Sprinkle crackers on top; dot with butter.
2. Cover and cook on high for 2½-3 hours. Sprinkle with remaining cheese. Cook 10 minutes longer or until the cheese is melted.

SPANISH HOMINY

I received this recipe from a good friend who is a fabulous cook. The colorful side dish gets its zesty flavor from spicy canned tomatoes with green chilies.
—Donna Brockett Kingfisher, OK

Prep: 15 min. • **Cook:** 6 hours
Makes: 12 servings

- **4 cans (15½ ounces each) hominy, rinsed and drained**
- **1 can (14½ ounces) diced tomatoes, undrained**
- **1 can (10 ounces) diced tomatoes and green chilies, undrained**
- **1 can (8 ounces) tomato sauce**
- **¾ pound sliced bacon, diced**
- **1 large onion, chopped**
- **1 medium green pepper, chopped**

1. In a 5-qt. slow cooker, combine the hominy, tomatoes and tomato sauce.
2. In a large skillet, cook bacon until crisp; remove with a slotted spoon to paper towels. Drain the fat, reserving 1 tablespoon drippings.
3. In the same skillet, saute onion and green pepper in drippings until tender. Stir onion mixture and bacon into hominy mixture. Cover and cook mixture on low for 6-8 hours or until heated through.

SPANISH HOMINY

VEGETABLE-STUFFED PEPPERS

I like to fix meatless main dishes for a change of pace. This one has become a monthly mainstay for my family. Filling green peppers is an appealing way to deliver a flavorful combination of cooked rice, kidney beans, corn and onions.
—Sandra Allen Austin, TX

Prep: 10 min. • **Cook:** 8¼ hours
Makes: 6 servings

- **2 cans (14½ ounces each) diced tomatoes, undrained**
- **1 can (16 ounces) kidney beans, rinsed and drained**
- **1½ cups cooked rice**
- **2 cups shredded cheddar cheese, divided**
- **1 package (10 ounces) frozen corn, thawed**
- **¼ cup chopped onion**
- **1 teaspoon Worcestershire sauce**
- **¾ teaspoon chili powder**
- **½ teaspoon pepper**
- **¼ teaspoon salt**
- **6 medium green peppers**

1. In a large bowl, combine the tomatoes, beans, rice, 1½ cups cheese, corn, onion, Worcestershire sauce, chili powder, pepper and salt. Remove and discard tops and seeds of green peppers. Fill each pepper with about 1 cup vegetable mixture. Place in a 5-qt. slow cooker. Cover and cook on low for 8 hours.
2. Sprinkle with remaining cheese. Cover and cook 15 minutes longer or until peppers are tender and cheese is melted.

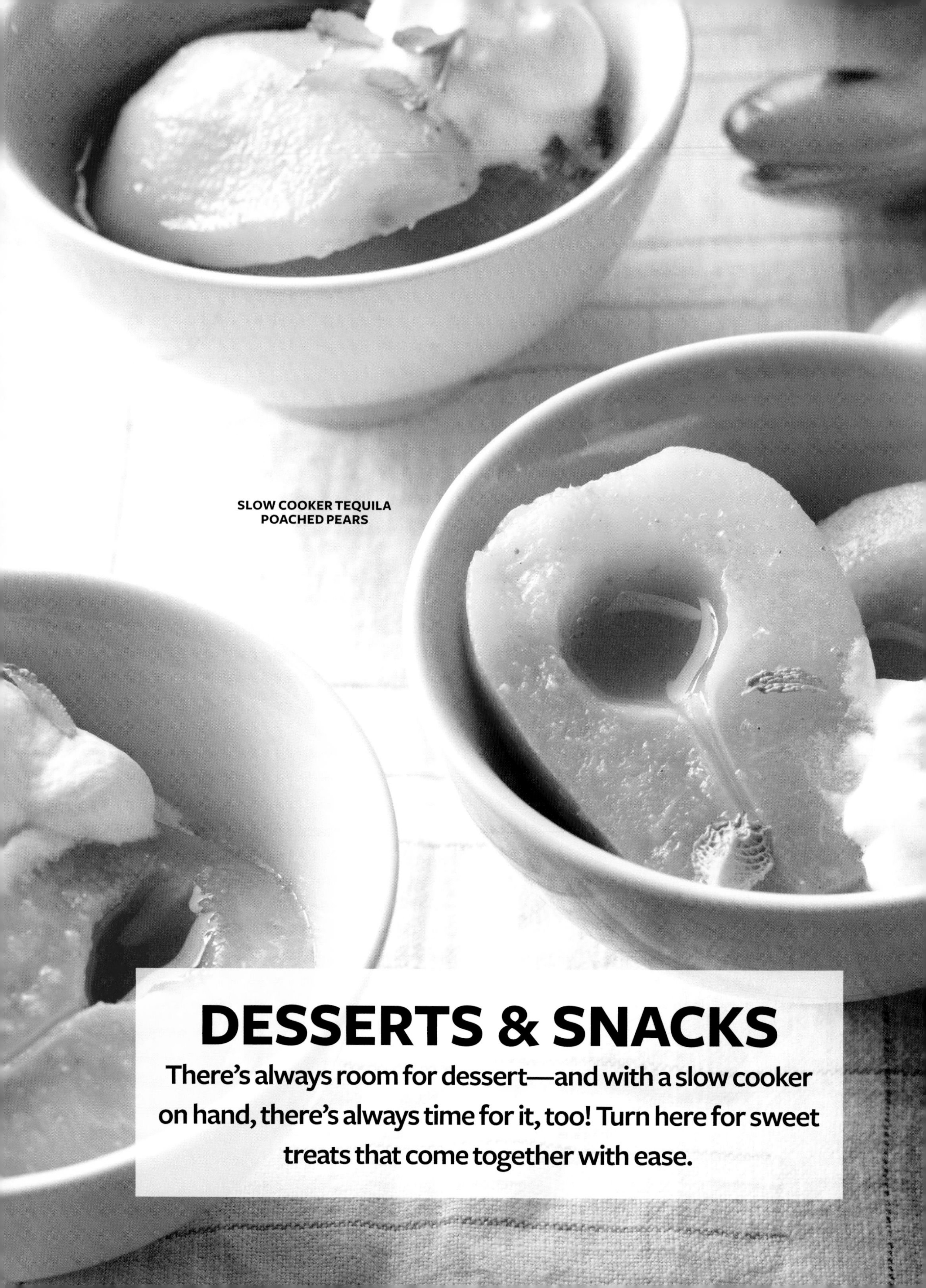

SLOW COOKER TEQUILA POACHED PEARS

DESSERTS & SNACKS

There's always room for dessert—and with a slow cooker on hand, there's always time for it, too! Turn here for sweet treats that come together with ease.

SLOW COOKER TEQUILA POACHED PEARS

Bring out this creative dish when you want to impress dinner guests. It's a unique dessert to make with tequila, but it is deliciously refreshing with fresh pears and a little mint.

—**Nancy Heishman** Las Vegas, NV

Prep: 20 min. • **Cook:** 4 hours
Makes: 8 servings

- **2 cups water**
- **1 can (11.3 ounces) pear nectar**
- **1 cup tequila**
- **½ cup sugar**
- **2 tablespoons lime juice**
- **2 teaspoons grated lime peel**
- **1 cinnamon stick (3 inches)**
- **¼ teaspoon ground nutmeg**
- **8 whole Anjou pears, peeled**
- **Sweetened whipped cream**
- **Fresh mint leaves**

1. In a large saucepan, combine the first eight ingredients. Bring to a boil over medium-high heat; boil 2 minutes, stirring constantly.
2. Place pears in a 4- or 5-qt. slow cooker; add liquid. Cook, covered, on low until tender, 4-5 hours. Remove cinnamon stick and discard. Pour 3 cups cooking liquid in a small saucepan. Bring to a boil; cook, uncovered, until liquid is reduced to 1 cup, about 20 minutes.
3. Halve pears lengthwise and core them. Serve with sauce, whipped cream and mint leaves.

DID YOU KNOW?

The skin on a pear can turn dark and tough when the pear is cooked. That's why many recipes call for the skin to be removed. Peel skin from a pear quickly and easily with a vegetable peeler.

BLACK & BLUE COBBLER

It never occurred to me that I could make a cobbler in my slow cooker. When I saw a few similar recipes, I decided to give it a try, using my favorite fruity dessert. It took a bit of experimenting, but the tasty results were well worth it.

—**Martha Creveling** Orlando, FL

Prep: 15 min. • **Cook:** 2 hours + standing
Makes: 6 servings

- **1 cup all-purpose flour**
- **1½ cups sugar, divided**
- **1 teaspoon baking powder**
- **¼ teaspoon salt**
- **¼ teaspoon ground cinnamon**
- **¼ teaspoon ground nutmeg**
- **2 large eggs, lightly beaten**
- **2 tablespoons whole milk**
- **2 tablespoons canola oil**
- **2 cups fresh or frozen blackberries**
- **2 cups fresh or frozen blueberries**
- **¾ cup water**
- **1 teaspoon grated orange peel**
- **Whipped cream or vanilla ice cream, optional**

1. In a large bowl, combine the flour, ¾ cup of the sugar, baking powder, salt, cinnamon and nutmeg. Combine the eggs, milk and oil; stir into dry ingredients just until moistened. Spread the batter evenly onto the bottom of a greased 5-qt. slow cooker.
2. In a large saucepan, combine the berries, water, orange peel and remaining sugar; bring to a boil. Remove from the heat; immediately pour over batter. Cover and cook on high for 2-2½ hours or until a toothpick inserted into the batter comes out clean.
3. Turn cooker off. Uncover and let stand for 30 minutes before serving. Serve with whipped cream or ice cream if desired.

SLOW-COOKED STRAWBERRY RHUBARB SAUCE

This tart and tangy fruit sauce is excellent over pound cake or ice cream. I've served the rosy-colored mixture many times and gotten rave reviews from friends and family. Try it and see what delicious ways you find to serve it.
—**Judith Wasman** Harkers Island, NC

Prep: 10 min. • **Cook:** 6 hours
Makes: 10 servings

- **6 cups chopped rhubarb (½-inch pieces)**
- **1 cup sugar**
- **½ teaspoon grated orange peel**
- **½ teaspoon ground ginger**
- **1 cinnamon stick (3 inches)**
- **½ cup white grape juice**
- **2 cups halved unsweetened strawberries**
- **Angel food cake, pound cake or vanilla ice cream**

1. Place rhubarb in a 3-qt. slow cooker. Combine sugar, orange peel and ginger; sprinkle over rhubarb. Add cinnamon stick and grape juice. Cover and cook on low for 5-6 hours or until rhubarb is tender.
2. Stir in strawberries; cook 1 hour longer. Discard cinnamon stick. Serve with cake or ice cream.

TROPICAL FRUIT COMPOTE

Have the taste of summer to relish all year long! To make a more adult version of this recipe, use brandy instead of the extra tropical fruit juice.
—***Taste of Home* Test Kitchen**

Prep: 15 min. • **Cook:** 2¼ hours
Makes: 6 servings

- **1 jar (23½ ounces) mixed tropical fruit**
- **1 jalapeno pepper, seeded and chopped**
- **¼ cup sugar**
- **1 tablespoon chopped crystallized ginger**
- **¼ teaspoon ground cinnamon**
- **1 can (15 ounces) mandarin oranges, drained**
- **1 jar (6 ounces) maraschino cherries, drained**
- **1 medium firm banana, sliced**
- **6 individual round sponge cakes**
- **6 tablespoons sweetened shredded coconut, toasted**

1. Drain tropical fruit, reserving ¼ cup liquid. Combine the tropical fruit and jalapeno in a 1½-qt. slow cooker.
2. 2. Combine the sugar, ginger, cinnamon and reserved juice; pour over fruit. Cover and cook on low for 2 hours. Stir in the mandarin oranges, cherries and banana; cook 15 minutes longer.
3. Place sponge cakes on dessert plates; top with compote. Sprinkle with coconut.

Note: Wear disposable gloves when cutting hot peppers; the oils can burn skin. Avoid touching your face.

INDULGENT COCONUT RICE PUDDING

This slow-cooked winter comfort dessert is a healthier option for your family that doesn't sacrifice comfort or flavor. If you can't find turbinado or raw sugar, you can use brown sugar, adjusting to ¾ cup. This can also be made in the oven if you'd like to experiment a bit.
—Teri Rasey Cadillac, MI

Prep: 10 min. • **Cook:** 4 hours
Makes: 12 servings

- **1 cup uncooked long grain rice**
- **5 cups coconut milk, divided**
- **2 tablespoons coconut oil**
- **1 cup turbinado (washed raw) sugar**
- **1 cup dried cranberries**
- **2 teaspoons vanilla extract**
- **1 teaspoon ground cinnamon**
- **Dash salt**
- **Toasted sweetened shredded coconut and additional coconut milk, optional**

Place rice in a 3- or 4-qt. slow cooker coated with cooking spray; pour in 4 cups coconut milk. Add coconut oil; distribute evenly over top. Add next five ingredients. Cook, covered, on low until rice is tender, 4-5 hours, adding enough remaining coconut milk to reach desired consistency. Let stand, uncovered, for 10 minutes. Serve warm, with toasted coconut and additional coconut milk if desired.

*

TEST KITCHEN TIP

It's easy to dress up the pudding. For even more tropical flair, top it with fresh bananas right before serving. You can give it some crunch by topping it with slivered almonds, chopped walnuts or hazelnuts. You can also try different flavors inspired by food from other countries. For instance, sprinkle the pudding with cardamom and top with golden raisins for a taste of India. For Thai-inspired flavor, after cooking, stir in fresh mint and fruit such as mangoes and kiwis.

INDULGENT COCONUT RICE PUDDING

CHOCOLATE ESPRESSO LAVA CAKE

My aunt inspired this cake, which can satisfy even the strongest chocolate craving. It's gooey and saucy but not crazy sweet—and it's potluck-perfect.
—Lisa Renshaw Kansas City, MO

Prep: 15 min. • **Cook:** 3 hours + standing
Makes: 16 servings

- **1 package chocolate fudge cake mix (regular size)**
- **1 tablespoon instant espresso powder**
- **3 cups 2% milk**
- **1 package (3.9 ounces) instant chocolate pudding mix**
- **1 cup (6 ounces) semisweet chocolate chips**
- **1 cup white baking chips**

1. Prepare cake mix batter according to package directions, adding espresso powder before mixing. Transfer to a greased 4-qt. slow cooker.
2. In a small bowl, whisk milk and pudding mix for 2 minutes. Let stand until soft-set, about 2 minutes. Pour over batter. Cook, covered, on low 3-3½ hours or until a toothpick inserted in cake portion comes out with moist crumbs.
3. Sprinkle top with chocolate chips and baking chips. Turn off slow cooker; remove insert. Let stand, uncovered, until chips are softened, 15-30 minutes. Serve warm.

SLOW COOKER
BERRY COBBLER

SLOW COOKER BERRY COBBLER

During warm weather, you can still enjoy the amazing flavor of homemade cobbler without heating up the kitchen.

—Karen Jarocki Yuma, AZ

Prep: 15 min. • **Cook:** 1¾ hours
Makes: 8 servings

- **1¼ cups all-purpose flour, divided**
- **2 tablespoons plus 1 cup sugar, divided**
- **1 teaspoon baking powder**
- **¼ teaspoon ground cinnamon**
- **1 large egg**
- **¼ cup fat-free milk**
- **2 tablespoons canola oil**
- **⅛ teaspoon salt**
- **2 cups fresh or frozen raspberries, thawed**
- **2 cups fresh or frozen blueberries, thawed**
- **Low-fat vanilla frozen yogurt, optional**

1. Whisk together 1 cup of the flour, 2 tablespoons sugar, baking powder and cinnamon. In another bowl, whisk together egg, milk and oil; add to dry ingredients, stirring just until moistened (batter will be thick). Spread onto bottom of a 5-qt. slow cooker coated with cooking spray.
2. Mix salt and the remaining flour and sugar; toss with berries. Spoon over batter. Cook, covered, on high until berry mixture is bubbly, 1¾-2 hours. If desired, serve with frozen yogurt.

SLOW COOKER FLAN IN A JAR

Spoil yourself or the people you love with these delightful portable custards. They're a cute and fun take on the Mexican dessert classic. Tuck a jar into your lunchbox for a sweet treat.

—Megumi Garcia Milwaukee, WI

Prep: 25 min. • **Cook:** 2 hours + cooling
Makes: 6 servings

- **½ cup sugar**
- **1 tablespoon plus 3 cups hot water (110°-115°)**
- **6 canning jars (4 ounces each) with lids and bands**
- **1 cup coconut or whole milk**
- **⅓ cup whole milk**
- **⅓ cup sweetened condensed milk**
- **2 large eggs plus 1 large egg yolk, lightly beaten**
- **Pinch salt**
- **1 teaspoon vanilla extract**
- **1 teaspoon dark rum, optional**

1. In a small heavy saucepan, spread sugar; cook, without stirring, over medium-low heat until it begins to melt. Gently drag melted sugar to center of pan so sugar melts evenly. Cook, stirring constantly, until melted sugar turns a deep amber color, about 2 minutes. Immediately remove from heat and carefully stir in 1 tablespoon hot water. Quickly pour into six hot 4-ounce jars.
2. In a small saucepan, heat coconut milk and whole milk until bubbles form around sides of pan; remove from heat. In a large bowl, whisk condensed milk, eggs, egg yolk and salt until blended but not foamy. Slowly stir in hot milk; stir in vanilla and, if desired, rum. Strain through a fine sieve. Pour egg mixture into prepared jars. Center lids on jars; screw on bands until fingertip tight.
3. Add remaining hot water to a 6-qt. slow cooker; place jars in slow cooker. Cook, covered, on high 2 hours or until centers are set. Cool 10 minutes on a wire rack. Remove jars to a 13x9-in. baking pan filled halfway with ice water; cool 10 minutes. Refrigerate until cold, about 1 hour. Run a knife around sides of jars; invert flans onto dessert plates.

SLOW COOKER FLAN IN A JAR

*

TEST KITCHEN TIP

You can use rum extract in place of the dark rum.

AMARETTO CHERRIES WITH DUMPLINGS

Treat everyone to a dessert of perfect comfort food—warm tart cherries drizzled with amaretto and topped with fluffy dumplings. A scoop of vanilla ice cream is the finishing touch.

—*Taste of Home* Test Kitchen

Prep: 15 min. • **Cook:** 7¾ hours
Makes: 6 servings

- **2 cans (14½ ounces each) pitted tart cherries**
- **¾ cup sugar**
- **¼ cup cornstarch**
- **⅛ teaspoon salt**
- **¼ cup amaretto or ½ teaspoon almond extract**

DUMPLINGS

- **1 cup all-purpose flour**
- **¼ cup sugar**
- **1 teaspoon baking powder**
- **½ teaspoon grated lemon peel**
- **⅛ teaspoon salt**
- **⅓ cup 2% milk**
- **3 tablespoons butter, melted**
- **Vanilla ice cream, optional**

1. Drain cherries, reserving ¼ cup juice. Place cherries in a 3-qt. slow cooker.
2. In a small bowl, mix sugar, cornstarch and salt; stir in reserved juice until smooth. Stir into cherries. Cook, covered, on high 7 hours. Drizzle amaretto over cherry mixture.
3. For dumplings, in a small bowl, whisk flour, sugar, baking powder, lemon peel and salt. In another bowl, whisk milk and melted butter. Add to flour mixture; stir just until moistened.
4. Drop by tablespoonfuls on top of hot cherry mixture. Cook, covered, for 45 minutes or until a toothpick inserted in center of dumplings comes out clean. If desired, serve warm with ice cream.

MOM'S HAZELNUT & CHOCOLATE BREAD PUDDING

Mom combined her love of hazelnut spread and bread pudding into one delicious recipe. I adapted it for my slow cooker to save time in the kitchen. It's a great make-ahead dessert.

—Jo Hahn Newport News, VA

Prep: 10 min. • **Cook:** 4 hours.
Makes: 12 servings

- **¼ cup unsalted butter**
- **2 tablespoons semisweet chocolate chips**
- **8 cups cubed challah or brioche**
- **½ cup chopped hazelnuts**
- **4 large eggs**
- **1½ cups fat-free milk**
- **½ cup fat-free half-and-half**
- **½ cup hazelnut spread**
- **¼ cup sugar**
- **½ teaspoon vanilla extract**
- **¼ teaspoon salt**
- **Heavy whipping cream, whipped**

1. Microwave butter and chocolate chips until melted, 30-45 seconds; stir until smooth. Cool. In a 3- or 4-qt. slow cooker coated with cooking spray, combine bread cubes and hazelnuts. In a large bowl, combine next seven ingredients, mixing well. Add chocolate mixture to bowl; whisk until smooth.
2. Pour egg mixture over bread and hazelnuts, gently pressing bread cubes to help them absorb liquid. Cook, covered, on low until a knife inserted in center comes out clean, 4-5 hours. Serve warm, dolloped with whipped cream.

TEST KITCHEN TIP

If you don't have challah or brioche bread, raisin bread is a tasty substitute. For testing, we used Nutella hazelnut spread. This decadent dessert is surprisingly low in fat and calories, so grab a spoon and dig in!

MOM'S HAZELNUT & CHOCOLATE BREAD PUDDING

SLOW-COOKED BLUEBERRY GRUNT

If you love blueberries, then you can't go wrong with this easy slow-cooked sweet. Serve it warm, and for a special treat, top it with a scoop of vanilla ice cream.
—Cleo Gonske Redding, CA

Prep: 20 min. • **Cook:** 2½ hours
Makes: 6 servings

- **4 cups fresh or frozen blueberries**
- **¾ cup sugar**
- **½ cup water**
- **1 teaspoon almond extract**

DUMPLINGS

- **2 cups all-purpose flour**
- **4 teaspoons baking powder**
- **1 teaspoon sugar**
- **½ teaspoon salt**
- **1 tablespoon cold butter**
- **1 tablespoon shortening**
- **¾ cup 2% milk**
- **Vanilla ice cream, optional**

1. Place blueberries, sugar, water and extract in a 3-qt. slow cooker; stir to combine. Cook, covered, on high for 2-3 hours or until bubbly.
2. For dumplings, in a small bowl, whisk flour, baking powder, sugar and salt. Cut in the butter and shortening until crumbly. Add milk; stir just until a soft dough forms.
3. Drop dough by tablespoonfuls on top of hot blueberry mixture. Cook, covered, 30 minutes longer or until a toothpick inserted in center of dumplings comes out clean. If desired, serve warm with vanilla ice cream.

ELVIS' PUDDING CAKE

I love the flavors of peanut butter and banana together, and this slow cooker pudding cake is just like eating an Elvis sandwich, only sweeter! Banana chips add a surprisingly crunchy texture; find them near the dried fruit in your grocery store.
—Lisa Renshaw Kansas City, MO

Prep: 10 min. • **Cook:** 3 hours + standing
Makes: 12 servings

- **3 cups cold 2% milk**
- **1 package (3.4 ounces) instant banana cream pudding mix**
- **1 package banana cake mix (regular size)**
- **½ cup creamy peanut butter**
- **2 cups peanut butter chips**
- **1 cup chopped dried banana chips**

1. In a small bowl, whisk the milk and pudding mix for 2 minutes. Let stand until soft-set, about 2 minutes. Transfer to a greased 5-qt. slow cooker.
2. Prepare cake mix batter according to package directions, adding peanut butter before mixing. Pour over pudding. Cover and cook on low for 3-3½ hours or until a toothpick inserted in the center comes out with moist crumbs.
3. Sprinkle with peanut butter chips; cover and let stand until partially melted, 15-20 minutes. Top with banana chips.

TROPICAL CRANBERRY COBBLER

The sunny island flavors of pineapple and orange go so well with the tart cranberries in this Hawaiian-inspired dessert. It's a great way to celebrate summer, even when time is tight.
—**Jeanne Holt** Mendota Heights, MN

Prep: 20 min. • **Cook:** 4 hours + standing
Makes: 12 servings

- **2 cups fresh or frozen cranberries, thawed**
- **1 can (20 ounces) unsweetened pineapple tidbits, drained**
- **¾ cup sweetened shredded coconut**
- **¾ cup orange marmalade**
- **½ cup packed light brown sugar**
- **6 tablespoons butter, melted**

TOPPING
- **1 package yellow cake mix (regular size)**
- **1 package (3.4 ounces) instant coconut cream pudding mix**
- **4 large eggs**
- **¾ cup pineapple-orange juice**
- **½ cup butter, melted**
- **¼ cup packed light brown sugar**
- **1 teaspoon vanilla extract**
- **Whipped cream, optional**
- **¼ cup sweetened shredded coconut, toasted**

1. In a greased 6-qt. oval slow cooker, layer cranberries, pineapple and ¾ cup coconut. In a bowl, mix marmalade, brown sugar and melted butter; spoon evenly over fruit.
2. In a large bowl, combine first seven topping ingredients; beat on low speed 1 minute. Beat on medium 2 minutes. Pour over filling.
3. Cook, covered, on low until top springs back when lightly touched, about 4 hours. Turn off slow cooker. Remove insert; let stand 15 minutes before serving. If desired, serve with whipped cream. Sprinkle with toasted coconut.

*

TEST KITCHEN TIP

This is a cross between a cobbler, dump cake and upside-down cake, with a substantial cake layer. Adding a package of pudding mix makes this layer tender and moist. Be sure to use instant pudding mix, however, not cook-and-serve.

BREAD PUDDING WITH BOURBON SAUCE

There's nothing I like better than this soothing bread pudding. The bourbon sauce makes the dessert taste special, but you won't believe how easy it is to prepare. Try it tonight.

—Hope Johnson Youngwood, PA

Prep: 15 min. • **Cook:** 3 hours
Makes: 6 servings

- **3 large eggs**
- **1¼ cups 2% milk**
- **½ cup sugar**
- **3 teaspoons vanilla extract**
- **½ teaspoon ground cinnamon**
- **¼ teaspoon ground nutmeg**
- **⅛ teaspoon salt**
- **4½ cups day-old cubed brioche or egg bread**
- **1¼ cups raisins**

BOURBON SAUCE

- **¼ cup butter, cubed**
- **½ cup sugar**
- **¼ cup light corn syrup**
- **3 tablespoons bourbon**

1. In a large bowl, whisk together first seven ingredients; stir in bread and raisins. Transfer to a greased 4-qt. slow cooker. Cook, covered, on low 3 hours. (To avoid scorching, rotate slow cooker insert one-half turn midway through cooking, lifting carefully with oven mitts.)
2. For sauce, place butter, sugar and corn syrup in a small saucepan; bring to a boil, stirring occasionally. Cook and stir until sugar is dissolved. Remove from heat; stir in bourbon. Serve warm with bread pudding.

Health tip: This dessert is rich even without the sauce. Skip it and save nearly 200 calories and 8 grams of fat.

BREAD PUDDING WITH BOURBON SAUCE

(5) INGREDIENTS

BUTTERSCOTCH FRUIT DIP

If you like the sweetness of butterscotch chips, you'll enjoy this warm rum-flavored fruit dip. I serve it with apple and pear wedges. It holds up for up to two hours in the slow cooker.

—Jeaune Hadl Van Meter Lexington, KY

Prep: 5 min. • **Cook:** 45 min.
Makes: about 3 cups

- **2 packages (10 to 11 ounces each) butterscotch chips**
- **⅔ cup evaporated milk**
- **⅔ cup chopped pecans**
- **1 tablespoon rum extract**
- **Apple and pear wedges**

In a 1½-qt. slow cooker, combine butterscotch chips and milk. Cover and cook on low for 45-50 minutes or until chips are softened; stir until smooth. Stir in pecans and extract. Serve dip warm with fruit.

SLOW COOKER KEY LIME FONDUE

Love fondue but want something other than milk chocolate? Dip into my silky white chocolate Key lime fondue with graham crackers, fresh fruit and cubed pound cake.

—**Elisabeth Larsen** Pleasant Grove, UT

Prep: 5 min. • **Cook:** 50 min.
Makes: 3 cups

- **1 can (14 ounces) sweetened condensed milk**
- **12 ounces white baking chocolate, finely chopped**
- **½ cup Key lime or regular lime juice**
- **1 tablespoon grated lime peel**
- **Graham crackers, macaroon cookies, fresh strawberries and sliced ripe bananas**

1. In a 1½-qt. slow cooker, combine milk, white chocolate and lime juice.
2. Cook, covered, on low 50-60 minutes or until chocolate is melted. Stir in lime peel. Serve dip with graham crackers, cookies and fruit.

*

TEST KITCHEN TIP

Get creative with dippers for this fondue. Consider cubed angel food cake, shortbread cookies, biscotti or marshmallows. Fruit options could include cantaloupe pieces, orange segments and pineapple chunks. If setting the fondue out for a party, you might want to brush cut fruit with lemon juice to prevent browning.

SLOW COOKER CHOCOLATE LAVA CAKE

Everyone who tries this dessert falls in love with it. Using a slow cooker liner makes cleanup a breeze.

—**Latona Dwyer** Palm Beach Gardens, FL

Prep: 15 min. • **Cook:** 3 hours
Makes: 12 servings

- **1 package devil's food cake mix (regular size)**
- **1⅔ cups water**
- **3 large eggs**
- **⅓ cup canola oil**
- **2 cups cold 2% milk**
- **1 package (3.9 ounces) instant chocolate pudding mix**
- **2 cups (12 ounces) semisweet chocolate chips**

1. In a large bowl, combine the cake mix, water, eggs and oil; beat on low speed for 30 seconds. Beat on medium for 2 minutes. Transfer to a greased 4-qt. slow cooker.
2. In another bowl, whisk milk and pudding mix for 2 minutes. Let stand until soft-set, about 2 minutes. Spoon over cake batter; sprinkle with chocolate chips. Cover and cook on high 3-4 hours or until a toothpick inserted in cake portion comes out with moist crumbs. Serve warm.

SLOW COOKER
KEY LIME FONDUE

MINTY HOT FUDGE SUNDAE CAKE

The best part about dessert from the slow cooker is that when dinner's done, a hot treat is ready to serve. In this case, it's a chocolaty, gooey, minty treat!

—Terri McKitrick Delafield, WI

Prep: 15 min. • **Cook:** 4 hours
Makes: 12 servings

- **1¾ cups packed brown sugar, divided**
- **1 cup all-purpose flour**
- **5 tablespoons baking cocoa, divided**
- **2 teaspoons baking powder**
- **½ teaspoon salt**
- **½ cup evaporated milk**
- **2 tablespoons butter, melted**
- **½ teaspoon vanilla extract**
- **⅛ teaspoon almond extract**
- **1 package (4.67 ounces) mint Andes candies**
- **1¾ cups boiling water**
- **4 teaspoons instant coffee granules**
- **Vanilla ice cream, whipped cream and maraschino cherries**

1. In a large bowl, combine 1 cup of the brown sugar, flour, 3 tablespoons cocoa, baking powder and salt. In another bowl, combine the milk, butter and extracts. Stir into dry ingredients just until moistened. Transfer to a 3-qt. slow cooker coated with cooking spray. Sprinkle with candies.
2. Combine the water, coffee granules and remaining brown sugar and cocoa; pour over batter (do not stir). Cover and cook on high for 4-4½ hours or until a toothpick inserted in the center of the cake comes out clean. Serve with ice cream, whipped cream and cherries.

WARM FRUIT SALAD

(5) INGREDIENTS

WARM FRUIT SALAD

I use canned goods and my slow cooker to whip up an old-fashioned treat that's loaded with sweet fruits. It makes a cozy dessert or even a change-of-pace side dish for large parties.

—Mary Ann Jonns Midlothian, IL

Prep: 10 min. • **Cook:** 2 hours
Makes: 14-18 servings

- **2 cans (29 ounces each) sliced peaches, drained**
- **2 cans (29 ounces each) pear halves, drained and sliced**
- **1 can (20 ounces) pineapple chunks, drained**
- **1 can (15¼ ounces) apricot halves, drained and sliced**
- **1 can (21 ounces) cherry pie filling**

In a 5-qt. slow cooker, combine the peaches, pears, pineapple and apricots. Top with pie filling. Cover and cook on high for 2 hours or until heated through. Serve with a slotted spoon.

(5) INGREDIENTS

BLUEBERRY COBBLER

This simple slow-cooked dessert comes together in a jiffy. If you like, you can substitute apple or cherry pie filling for the blueberry.

—Nelda Cronbaugh Belle Plaine, IA

Prep: 10 min. • **Cook:** 3 hours
Makes: 6 servings

- **1 can (21 ounces) blueberry pie filling**
- **1 package (9 ounces) yellow cake mix**
- **¼ cup chopped pecans**
- **¼ cup butter, melted**
- **Vanilla ice cream, optional**

Place pie filling in a greased 1½-qt. slow cooker. Sprinkle with cake mix and pecans. Drizzle with butter. Cover and cook on high for 3 hours or until topping is golden brown. Serve warm with ice cream if desired.

VERY VANILLA SLOW COOKER CHEESECAKE

Cinnamon and vanilla give this cheesecake so much flavor, and making it in the slow cooker creates a silky, smooth texture that's hard to resist.

—**Krista Lanphier** Milwaukee, WI

Prep: 40 min. • **Cook:** 2 hours + chilling
Makes: 6 servings

- **¾ cup graham cracker crumbs**
- **1 tablespoon sugar plus ⅔ cup sugar, divided**
- **¼ teaspoon ground cinnamon**
- **2½ tablespoons butter, melted**
- **2 packages (8 ounces each) cream cheese, softened**
- **½ cup sour cream**
- **2 to 3 teaspoons vanilla extract**
- **2 large eggs, lightly beaten**

TOPPING

- **2 ounces semisweet chocolate, chopped**
- **1 teaspoon shortening**
- **Miniature peanut butter cups or toasted sliced almonds**

1. Grease a 6-in. springform pan; place on a double thickness of heavy-duty foil (about 12 in. square). Wrap foil securely around pan.
2. Pour 1 in. water into a 6-qt. slow cooker. Layer two 24-in. pieces of foil. Starting with a long side, roll up foil to make a 1-in.-wide strip; shape into a circle. Place in bottom of slow cooker to make a rack.
3. In a small bowl, mix cracker crumbs, 1 tablespoon sugar and cinnamon; stir in butter. Press onto bottom and about 1 in. up sides of prepared pan.
4. In a large bowl, beat cream cheese and remaining sugar until smooth. Beat in sour cream and vanilla. Add eggs; beat on low speed just until combined. Pour into crust.
5. Place springform pan on foil circle without touching slow cooker sides. Cover slow cooker with a double layer of white paper towels; place lid securely over towels. Cook, covered, on high for 2 hours.
6. Do not remove lid; turn off slow cooker and let cheesecake stand, covered, in slow cooker 1 hour.
7. Remove springform pan from slow cooker; remove foil around pan. Cool cheesecake on a wire rack 1 hour longer. Loosen sides from pan with a knife. Refrigerate overnight, covering when completely cooled.
8. For topping, in a microwave, melt chocolate and shortening; stir until smooth. Cool slightly. Remove rim from springform pan. Pour chocolate mixture over cheesecake; sprinkle with miniature peanut butter cups or almonds.

To make ahead: Cheesecake may be stored in the refrigerator 4-6 days before serving. Wrap securely before chilling; top just before serving.

Note: Six-inch springform pans are available from Wilton Industries. Visit *wilton.com* or call 800-794-5866.

VERY VANILLA SLOW COOKER CHEESECAKE

★★★★★ **READER REVIEW**

"This cheesecake was awesome! So smooth and velvety that even my husband, who is not a cheesecake fan, loved it. A definite keeper that I will make again."

SANDYDENT TASTEOFHOME.COM

STRAWBERRY-BANANA PUDDING CAKE

This luscious pink pudding cake is so easy to put together. Serve it with ice cream and fresh fruit, and you'll have one very happy family.
—**Nadine Mesch** Mount Healthy, OH

Prep: 15 min. • **Cook:** 3½ hours + standing
Makes: 10 servings

- **1 package strawberry cake mix (regular size)**
- **1 package (3.4 ounces) instant banana cream pudding mix**
- **2 cups plain Greek yogurt**
- **4 large eggs**
- **1 cup water**
- **¾ cup canola oil**
- **2 tablespoons minced fresh basil**
- **1 cup white baking chips**
- **Optional toppings: vanilla ice cream, sliced bananas, sliced strawberries and fresh basil**

1. In a large bowl, combine first six ingredients; beat on low speed for 30 seconds. Beat on medium 2 minutes; stir in basil. Transfer to a greased 5-qt. slow cooker. Cook, covered, on low until edges of cake are golden brown (center will be moist), 3½-4 hours.
2. Turn off slow cooker; sprinkle cake with baking chips. Remove insert; let stand, uncovered, 10 minutes before serving. Serve warm with the toppings as desired.

STRAWBERRY-BANANA PUDDING CAKE

CHERRY & SPICE RICE PUDDING

I live in Traverse City, the Cherry Capital of the World, and what better way to celebrate our wonderful orchards than by using plump, tart dried cherries in my favorite desserts? This slow-cooked rice pudding recipe always turns out perfectly.
—**Deb Perry** Traverse City, MI

Prep: 10 min. • **Cook:** 2 hours
Makes: 12 servings

- **4 cups cooked long grain rice**
- **1 can (12 ounces) evaporated milk**
- **1 cup 2% milk**
- **⅓ cup sugar**
- **¼ cup water**
- **¾ cup dried cherries**
- **3 tablespoons butter, softened**
- **2 teaspoons vanilla extract**
- **½ teaspoon ground cinnamon**
- **¼ teaspoon ground nutmeg**

1. In a large bowl, combine the rice, evaporated milk, milk, sugar and water. Stir in remaining ingredients. Transfer to a 3-qt. slow cooker coated with cooking spray.
2. Cover and cook on low for 2-3 hours or until mixture is thickened. Stir lightly before serving. Serve warm or cold. Refrigerate leftovers.

(5) INGREDIENTS

CHOCOLATE PEANUT DROPS

I got this recipe from a friend. I was surprised to learn these chocolaty candies came from a slow cooker. You can get several dozen candies from one batch.

—Anita Bell Hermitage, TN

Prep: 20 min. • **Cook:** 1½ hours + standing
Makes: about 11 dozen

- **4 ounces German sweet chocolate, chopped**
- **1 package (12 ounces) semisweet chocolate chips**
- **4 packages (10 to 12 ounces each) white baking chips**
- **2 jars (16 ounces each) lightly salted dry roasted peanuts**

1. In a 6-qt. slow cooker, layer the ingredients in order listed (do not stir). Cover and cook on low for 1½ hours. Stir to combine. (If chocolate is not melted, cover and cook 15 minutes longer; stir. Repeat in 15-minute increments until chocolate is melted.)
2. Drop mixture by rounded tablespoonfuls onto waxed paper. Let stand until set. Store in an airtight container at room temperature.

Chocolate Peanut Bark: Cook the chocolate mixture as directed; spread into two 15x10x1-in. waxed paper-lined baking pans. Refrigerate until firm, about 30 minutes. Cut into bite-sized pieces.

★★★★★ **READER REVIEW**

"This was the best-tasting candy I have ever made. I always favor the peanut clusters from the store, but these are even better. So creamy and smooth they just melt in your mouth."

SMELONAS TASTEOFHOME.COM

PINEAPPLE UPSIDE
DOWN DUMP CAKE

PINEAPPLE UPSIDE-DOWN DUMP CAKE

No matter what the season, this dump cake recipe is wonderful! It works well with gluten-free and sugar-free cake mixes as well.

—Karin Gatewood Dallas, TX

Prep: 10 min. • **Cook:** 2 hours + standing
Makes: 10 servings

- **¾ cup butter, divided**
- **⅔ cup packed brown sugar**
- **1 jar (6 ounces) maraschino cherries, drained**
- **½ cup chopped pecans, toasted**
- **1 can (20 ounces) unsweetened pineapple tidbits or crushed pineapple, undrained**
- **1 package yellow cake mix (regular size)**
- **Vanilla ice cream, optional**

1. In a microwave, melt ½ cup butter; stir in brown sugar. Spread evenly onto bottom of a greased 5-qt. slow cooker. Sprinkle with cherries and pecans; top with pineapple. Sprinkle evenly with dry cake mix. Melt remaining butter; drizzle over top.
2. Cook, covered, on high until fruit mixture is bubbly, about 2 hours. (To avoid scorching, rotate slow cooker insert one-half turn midway through cooking, lifting carefully with oven mitts.)
3. Turn off slow cooker; let stand, uncovered, 30 minutes before serving. If desired, serve with ice cream.

Note: To toast nuts, bake in a shallow pan in a 350° oven for 5-10 minutes or cook in a skillet over low heat until lightly browned, stirring occasionally.

SLOW COOKER PEACH CRUMBLE

SLOW COOKER PEACH CRUMBLE

I look forward to going on our beach vacation every year, but I don't always relish the time spent cooking for everybody. This slow cooker dessert (or breakfast!) gives me more time to lie in the sun and enjoy the waves. Melty ice cream is a must.

—Colleen Delawder Herndon, VA

Prep: 20 min. • **Cook:** 3 hours
Makes: 8 servings

- **1 tablespoon butter, softened**
- **6 large ripe peaches, peeled and sliced (about 6 cups)**
- **2 tablespoons light brown sugar**
- **1 tablespoon lemon juice**
- **1 tablespoon vanilla extract**
- **2 tablespoons coconut rum, optional**

TOPPING

- **1 cup all-purpose flour**
- **¾ cup packed light brown sugar**
- **1½ teaspoons baking powder**
- **1 teaspoon ground cinnamon**
- **½ teaspoon baking soda**
- **⅛ teaspoon salt**
- **1 cup old-fashioned oats**
- **6 tablespoons cold butter, cubed**

1. Grease a 6-qt. oval slow cooker with 1 tablespoon softened butter. Toss peaches with brown sugar, lemon juice, vanilla and, if desired, rum; spread evenly in slow cooker.
2. Whisk together first six topping ingredients; stir in oats. Cut in butter until crumbly; sprinkle over peaches. Cook, covered, on low until peaches are tender, 3-4 hours.

RECIPE INDEX